A Workbook for Carlson's

PHYSIOLOGY OF BEHAVIOR

Second Edition

Leanna J. Standish

Smith College

Allyn and Bacon, Inc.
Boston   London   Sydney   Toronto

Production Editor: Wendy Ritger

ISBN: 0-205-07264-X

Printed in the United States of America.

10 9 8 7 6 5 4 3 2   86 85 84 83 82

CREDITS

Most figures in this Workbook are adapted from those in Carlson's text, PHYSIOLOGY OF BEHAVIOR, Second Edition. We also wish to acknowledge the following authors and publishers who granted permission for use of their materials.

Figure, p. 72 - Adapted with permission from McGraw-Hill Book Co. from THE HUMAN NERVOUS SYSTEM, 2nd edition, by Noback and Demarest. Copyright 1975, by McGraw-Hill, Inc. Figure, p. 114 - Redrawn by permission of the Royal Society and the authors from Dowling, J.E., and Boycott, B.B., PROCEEDINGS OF THE ROYAL SOCIETY (LONDON), 1966, Series B, 166, 80-111. Figures, pp. 121 and 122 - Adapted from Ades, H.W., and Engström, H., Form and innervation in the vestibular epithelia. In THE ROLE OF THE VESTIBULAR ORGANS IN THE EXPLORATION OF SPACE, edited by A. Graybill. U.S. Naval School of Medicine: NASA SP-77, 1965. Figures, pp. 125, 126, and 166 - Adapted from Bloom and Fawcett, A TEXTBOOK OF HISTOLOGY. Philadelphia: W.B. Saunders, 1968. Figure, p. 138 - Adapted with permission from McGraw-Hill Book Co. from THE HUMAN NERVOUS SYSTEM, 2nd edition, by Noback and Demarest. Copyright 1975, by McGraw-Hill, Inc. Figure, p. 150 - From Rose, J.E., Brugge, J.F., Anderson, D.J., and Hind, J.E., JOURNAL OF NEUROPHYSIOLOGY, 1967, 30, 769-793. Figure, p. 154 - Adapted from Noback, C.R., and Demarest, R.J., THE NERVOUS SYSTEM: INTRODUCTION AND REVIEW. New York: McGraw-Hill, 1972. Figure, p. 155 - Adapted from Noback, C.R., and Demarest, R.J., THE NERVOUS SYSTEM: INTRODUCTION AND REVIEW. New York: McGraw-Hill, 1972. Figure, p. 163 - Adapted from Crosby, E.C., Humphrey, T., and Lauer, E.W., CORRELATIVE ANATOMY OF THE NERVOUS SYSTEM. New York: Macmillan, 1962.

Figure, p. 173 - Adapted with permission from McGraw-Hill Book Co. from THE HUMAN NERVOUS SYSTEM, 2nd edition, by Noback and Demarest. Copyright 1975, by McGraw-Hill, Inc. Figure, p. 200 - Reproduced, with permission, from the ANNUAL REVIEW OF PSYCHOLOGY, Volume 14. © 1963 by Annual Reviews Inc. From O'Kelly, L.I., 57-92. Figure, p. 234 - From Hartmann, E., THE BIOLOGY OF DREAMING, 1967. Courtesy of Charles C. Thomas, Publisher, Springfield, Illinois. Figure, p. 238 - From Takahashi, Y. Growth hormone secretion related to the sleep waking rhythm. In THE FUNCTIONS OF SLEEP, edited by R. Drucker-Colin, M. Shkurovich, and M.B. Sterman. New York: Academic Press, 1979. Figure, p. 240 - Reprinted with permission from PHYSIOLOGY & BEHAVIOR, Volume 22, Rideout, B. Non-REM sleep as a source of learning deficits induced by REM sleep deprivation, Copyright 1979, Pergamon Press, Ltd, 1043-1047, Figures, p. 248 - From Bremer, F., BULLETIN DE L'ACADÉMIE ROYALE DE BELIGIQUE, 1937, 4, 68-86. Figure, p. 252, left - From Mouret, J.R., Bobillier, P., and Jouvet, M., EUROPEAN JOURNAL OF PHARMACOLOGY, 1968, 5, 17-22. Figure, p. 252, right - From Dement, W., Mitler, M., and Henriksen, S., REVUE CANADIENNE DE BIOLOGIE, Volume 31, Suppl., Printemps, 1972, 239-246. Figure, p. 298 - From Chorover, S.L., and Schiller, P.H., JOURNAL OF COMPARATIVE AND PHYSIOLOGICAL PSYCHOLOGY, 1965, 59, 73-78. Copyright 1965 by the American Psychological Association. Adapted by permission of the publisher and author. Figure, p. 332 - Redrawn from Bassuk, E.L., and Gerson, S. Deinstitutionalization and mental health services. SCIENTIFIC AMERICAN, 1978, 238, 46-53. Figure, p. 333 - From Snyder, S.H. JOURNAL OF CONTINUING EDUCATION IN PSYCHIATRY, 1978, 39, 21-33.

TABLE OF CONTENTS

To the Student

I have written this workbook to help you to learn physiological psychology. It is designed to facilitate your understanding of the information and concepts in Professor Carlson's text Physiology of Behavior. But "understanding" has only a vague meaning. In any course you are aware that you will be required to "understand" the material covered in the text and lectures, but often, nothing more is said by the instructor than that. Perhaps you have sadly discovered what "understanding" meant in mid-semester during your first major exam.

It is easy to confuse momentary understanding with real mastery of the material. This workbook will not only help you to master your text, but give you an objective criterion by which to measure your understanding. Both Neil Carlson and I agree that what is meant by understanding is what you are able to do. You should be able to give precise definitions of key terms in each chapter, answer study questions and speak and write fluently about each learning objective. After all, the ability to respond to questions and explain your answer is typically what we mean by "knowing".

This workbook involves your active participation. You must read, think and write answers. My objective is to take some of the mystique out of knowing and provide you with a programmatic self-paced method to learn about physiological psychology - and really learn about it, not just get the "gist" of each chapter.

Let me briefly explain the objectives and rationale for each of the five sections of each workbook chapter.

Essential Concepts

I have three purposes in this section. 1) Hopefully, the presentation of the major ideas of the chapter should motivate you to read the text assignment and answer the study questions. 2) These statements present the important ideas and facts of the text chapter in order to help you form an organizational framework into which you can place the specifics of each textbook chapter. 3) These essential concepts should help you to remember at a later time what you have learned.

Key Terms

As you probably already know, a large part of learning a new discipline involves the acquisition of the vocabulary of that discipline. You should be able to pronounce and supply precise definitions of each term listed. Next to each term is the page in the text where that term is defined.

Learning Objectives

Each learning objective specifies what you should be able to do as a function of reading and thinking about each section of the text. If you can fluently speak and/or write on each objective you can be certain that you are fully prepared for an exam and well on your way to becoming a professional physiological psychologist.

Study Questions

The study questions are the most important aspect of each workbook chapter. Each learning objective has a set of study questions to help you to achieve that objective. The study questions are designed to induce you to actively participate in what you are reading about. Since the study questions follow the order of presentation of textbook material and the relevant text pages are indicated after each, the answering of these questions should be relatively simple. Try not to echo the text, but rather, try to answer the question in your own well-thought-out words. I have tried to supply a study question for every important concept, experiment or piece of information covered in the text and figures. In other words, all the material is covered. Working through each workbook chapter should alleviate the need for taking notes on the text. Lastly, your own handwritten answers to these questions will make studying for quizzes and exams relatively easy and efficient. If you find you are becoming bored, take a break.

Thought Questions

Many of the textbook chapters discuss some interesting and important philosophical ideas. I have attempted to bring these to your attention in the thought questions. Often these questions will ask you to integrate information from previous chapters or speculate on a given issue. Few of these questions have correct answers. I would be interested to hear some of your answers. My address is below.

During this semester I would urge you to go about your job of learning physiological psychology in the following way.

1) Get an overview of the text chapter by reading the Essential Concepts.

2) Read the textbook chapter.

3) Answer all the study questions.

4) Write a short definition next to each Key Term.

5) Make sure you can speak and write fluently on all the Learning Objectives.

You have an excellent text, a programmatic study guide and a whole course in which to learn about the physiology of behavior. As you will discover, it is a fascinating topic. Good luck, and write to me if you have any comments, suggestions or advice on how to make this a better workbook.

Best wishes,

Leanna Standish
Psychology Department
Smith College
Northampton, Mass. 01063

1

Introduction

---

1. The aim of <u>physiological psychology</u> is to explain complex human behavior
    in terms of physiological mechanisms. For this reason, physiological
    psychologists need to know a great deal about both psychology (behavior)
    and physiology.

2. One form of scientific explanation consists of <u>reducing</u> or explaining
    complex behavioral phenomena in terms of simpler physical structures
    (i.e., cells) and events (i.e., electrical activity of brain cells).
    This means that we must understand "psychologically" why a particular
    behavior occurs before we can understand the physiological mechanisms
    that made it occur.

    How important is acceptance of evolution to our study of physiological psych?

3. The principle of <u>natural selection</u> shapes the thinking and research of
    physiological psychologists. We must always keep in mind that each
    behavioral trait and physiological mechanism of every species has
    evolved because it somehow increased the likelihood of survival and
    reproduction.

4. Self-awareness and langauge seem to give rise in humans to the belief in
    <u>free will</u>. <u>Physiological psychologists believe that the body (particu-
    larly the brain) controls our minds and our consciousness, not the other</u>
    way around. *The body influences our consciousness, but does it control it?*

5. Since we can only observe and measure energy and matter of the physical
    world, we must act like <u>determinists</u> in the laboratory despite our per-
    sonal philosophical or religious views on free will.

6. Humans experience a feeling of <u>unity of consciousness</u>. The fact that
    surgically severing the corpus callosum gives rise to two distinct
    minds strongly suggests that the unity of our conscious awareness is a
    product of the interconnections of various regions of the brain.

7. The brain receives <u>inputs</u> from both the external world and from inside the body itself. These inputs are of two types; <u>neural</u> and <u>chemical</u>. The brain controls behavior through its <u>outputs</u>; both neural and chemical.

Key Words

generalization (p. 2) *using particular instances as examples of general laws*

reduction (p. 2) *phenomena are explained in terms of simpler phenomena.*

principle of natural selection (p. 5) *that is evolution.*
the principle of natural selection guides the thinking of all physiological psychologists

determinism (p. 6) *that behavior will be explained down to the last detail when physiology is completely understood*

unity of consciousness (p. 7) *human awareness brings with it a feeling of unity of consciousness*

split brain operation (pp. 8-11) *division of right & left hemispheres causes two distinct awarenesses.*

neural input (p. 12) *sensory inputs.*

neural output (p. 12) *brain control of skeletal and smooth muscles (heart, gut & glands.*

LEARNING OBJECTIVES FOR CHAPTER 1

When you have mastered the material in the chapter, you will be able to:

①. Describe what the physiological psychologist means by explanation.

②. Explain how the principle of natural selection is relevant to physiological psychology.

③. Describe how the physiological psychologist deals with the question of free will vs. determinism

④. Describe what we know about the physiological basis of the "unity of consciousness".

5. List the neural and chemical inputs and outputs of the brain.

OBJECTIVE 1-1: Describe what the physiological psychologist means by explanation.

---

①. Define the two forms of scientific explanation. (p. 2)

Generalization: *making a general statement from observing specific cause and effects.*

Reduction: *Explain phenomena in terms of simpler phenomena*

(2). Why is the physiological psychologist usually concerned with reduction? (pp. 2,3)

(3). Describe the relationship between psychology and physiology in physiological psychology. (pp. 2,3)

(4). Give an example of how psychology directs the experiments of the physiological psychologist. (pp. 3,4)

(5). Give an example of how physiology can tell us something about psychology. (pp. 3,4)

OBJECTIVE 1-2: Explain how the principle of natural selection is relevant to physiological psychology.

6. List the steps showing how the theory of natural selection is the basis of biological evolution. (pp. 4,5)

(7). Give an original example showing how the principle of natural selection shapes the thinking and research of physiological psychologists. (p. 5)

> **OBJECTIVE 1-3:** Describe how the physiological psychologist deals
> with the question of free will vs. determinism.

8. What evidence do we have that consciousness is a physiological
function? (p. 5)

    *It is altered by changes in the structure or chemistry
    of the brain.*

9. How are self-awareness, communication and the belief in free will
interrelated? (p. 6)

10. Which is true of the determinist position on free will? (p. 6)

    The mind controls the brain or <u>the brain controls the mind</u>?

11. Why is it that we can only act like determinists in the laboratory,
despite our personal philosophical views on free will? (pp. 6,7)

    *because in investigating physical things, our explanations
    must be physical also.*

> **OBJECTIVE 1-4:** Describe what we know about the physiological
> bases of the "unity of consciousness".

12. What is it about the structure of the human brain that gives rise to
our experience of the "unity of consciousness"? (p. 7)

    *The fact that different aspects of consciousness depend on
    specific regions of the brain.
    The integration of information that is received by different sensory
    modalities appears to be accomplished by means of physical
    interconnections between the brain regions that perform those analyses.*

13. In <u>most</u> people, which hemisphere of the brain controls speech? Right
or (left)? (p. 8,9)

14. Explain how a "split brain" operation can give rise to two minds in one brain. (pp. 8,9,10)

When the corpus callosum is severed, each hemisphere of the brain seems to have its own mind independent of the other. That is that both hemispheres are able to receive sensory stimuli independently and to react to that stimuli in their own sphere of influence independently.

15. Explain why an amusing picture shown to the right hemisphere might produce laughter in a "split-brain patient" but that only the left hemisphere can know and answer the question, "Why are you laughing?". (pp. 8-11)

The right hemisphere is able to respond to visual stimuli and cause laughter, but only the left hemisphere which controls speech is able to respond audibly.

OBJECTIVE 1-5: List the neural and chemical inputs and outputs of the brain.

---

16. List the neural inputs to the brain. (p. 12)

List the nonneural inputs to the brain.

List the neural outputs from the brain.

List the nonneural outputs from the brain.

17. To which of the above four categories do each of the following physiological functions most belong? (p. 12)

     a. a visual stimulus *neural input*
     b. contraction of a skeletal muscle in the leg *neural output*

5

c. secretion of epinephrine _____

d. an increase in heart beat rate _*neural output*_

e. glucose in the blood _____

f. release of hormones in the anterior pituitary
   gland _*nonneural output*_

g. contraction of the smooth muscle of the large
   intestine _*neural output*_

h. release of estrogen from the ovary _*nonneural output*_ ?

One more thing............

18. When reading the text, when should you look at the figures? Why?
    (p. 14)

Thought Questions

1. Suppose, as a physiological psychologist, you were not a determinist
   and chose not to act so even in the laboratory. Suppose you believed
   that the mind and/or consciousness controls the brain, rather than the
   reverse. Can you devise any sensible research questions or methods
   that would help you to explore the relationship between consciousness
   and the brain?

2. What do you suppose is the survival value of our species' "unity of
   consciousness"? Why did it evolve? Why was this physiological function naturally selected?

3. Try to imagine what the human world would be like if everyone had a
   disconnected corpus callosum. Would we survive as a species? What
   would our culture be like?

4. We have argued that there are two kinds of inputs and outputs of the
   brain; neural and chemical. Could there be other types of inputs or
   outputs, the existence of which is yet unknown to us? What might
   their nature be?

2

The Cells of the Nervous System

Essential Concepts

1. The nervous system, like all other living tissue, is composed of cells. Neurons and glial cells are the basic elements of the nervous system. The neuron's basic function is to relay electrical and chemical messages. Glial cells, on the other hand, support, separate, insulate and metabolically sustain neurons.

2. Neurons possess organelles, such as mitochondria, endoplasmic reticulum, a nucleus and nucleolus, that are common to all cells. However, neurons, unlike other types of cells, have specialized processes, the axon, dendrite and terminal button. The axon transmits electrical messages to other neurons and dendrites receive information from other axons. In the case of sensory neurons, the dendrites of these cells interact directly with the outside world.

3. Myelin is formed by oligodendroglia in the central nervous system (CNS) and by Schwann cells in the peripheral nervous system (PNS). Myelin not only isolates axons from one another but allows for faster and more efficient electrical transmission. In the PNS, regrowth of axons can occur after nerve injury. This is not true for the CNS because the growth of scar tissue at the site of injury blocks budding axons and supporting cells do not guide their growth.

4. The CNS (brain and spinal cord) is chemically isolated from the rest of the body by the blood-brain barrier. Endothelial cells and one type of glial cell, astrocytes, surround capillaries of the CNS and permit only certain molecules to pass from the capillaries to the nervous system cells.

5. The blood-brain barrier is not uniform in all parts of the CNS. In one portion of the brain, the area postrema, certain molecules barred from entering the brain elsewhere cross through the capillary walls with relative ease. This small area is involved in the reflex of vomiting.

7

6. The blood-brain barrier works in reverse. Proteins present in the brain cannot enter the blood supply. It is thought that the disease <u>multiple sclerosis</u> results from a virus-produced damage to the blood-brain barrier. This breakdown of the barrier allows protein present in myelin to enter the entire body's blood supply. The immune system recognizes this myelin as foreign protein and builds antibodies against myelin. As a result, progressive destruction of myelin sheaths occurs, producing a loss of muscular control and abnormal sensory activity.

<u>Key Words</u>

membrane (p. 17)

cytoplasm (p. 18)

mitochondria (p. 18)

endoplasmic reticulum (p. 18)

ribosomes (p. 18)

Golgi apparatus (p. 18)

nucleus (p. 18)

nucleolus (p. 18)

chromosome (p. 18)

DNA (p. 18)

messenger RNA (p. 18)

microfilaments (p. 19)

microtubules (p. 19)

neurosecretory cell (p. 19)

soma (p. 20)

dendrite (p. 20)

synapse (p. 20)

axon (p. 20)

dendritic spine (p. 20)

terminal button (p. 22)

unipolar neuron (p. 22)

bipolar neuron (p. 22)

multipolar neuron (p. 22)

transmitter substance (p. 22)

neuroglia (p. 23)

astrocyte (p. 23)

phagocyte (p. 24)

microglia (p. 24)

oligodendroglia (p. 24)

myelin sheath (p. 24)

node of Ranvier (p. 24)

satellite cell (p. 26)

Schwann cell (p. 26)

blood-brain barrier (p. 28)

area postrema (p. 29)

experimental allergic encephalomyelitis (p. 29)

multiple sclerosis (p. 29)

LEARNING OBJECTIVES FOR CHAPTER 2

When you have mastered the material in the chapter, you will
be able to:

1. Draw a diagram of a typical animal cell indicating the location, appear-
    ance and function of all its major structures.

2. Describe the special structural features of neurons.

3. Describe the function of the two kinds of cells in the CNS: neurons and
    glia.

4. Name and distinguish the function of cells in the PNS from cells in the
    CNS.

5. Explain the function and cellular basis of the blood-brain barrier.

OBJECTIVE 2-1: Draw a diagram of a typical animal cell indicating the location, appearance and function of all its major structures.

1.

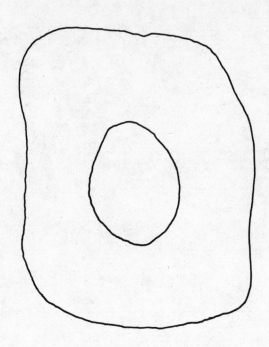

2. Match each cell structure on the left with its function on the right. (pp. 17,18,19)

_c_ 1. membrane

_f_ 2. mitochondria

_a_ 3. endoplasmic reticulum

_h_ 4. ribosome

_b_ 5. Golgi apparatus

_j_ 6. nucleolus

_e_ 7. chromosome

_g_ 8. DNA

_i_ 9. mRNA

_d_ 10. microtubules and microfilaments

a. transports and segregates molecules within the cytoplasm

b. packages molecules for secretion

c. contains specialized molecules that detect substances outside the cell.

d. gives structural framework to the cell and helps transport molecules within the cell

e. contains genetic information

f. involved in extraction of energy from breakdown of glucose

g. complex genetic molecules that make up chromosomes

h. involved in protein synthesis

i. travels to ribosomes where it causes protein synthesis

j. involved in the manufacture of ribosomes

```
┌─────────────────────────────────────────────────────────────────┐
│   OBJECTIVE 2-2:  Describe the special structural features of neurons. │
└─────────────────────────────────────────────────────────────────┘
```

3. Why are some neurons called neurosecretory cells? (p. 19)

4. Draw a diagram of a typical neuron indicating the function of the soma,
    dendrites, dendritic spines, axon and terminal buttons. (pp. 20-22)

```
┌─────────────────────────────────────────────────────────────────┐
│   OBJECTIVE 2-3:  Describe the function of the two kinds of cells in │
│                   the CNS:  neurons and glia.                     │
└─────────────────────────────────────────────────────────────────┘
```

5. How does the function of neurons and glia differ? (p. 23)
    *neurons transmit the neural impulses that make up behavior
    whereas the glia are support cells for neurons holding them in place
    and providing needed chemicals*

    How are neurons and glia interrelated? (p. 23)
    *glia supply neurons with chemicals that they need and insulate
    individual neurons from other neurons so that neural messages are not
    scrambled.*

6. List the three major functions of astroglia. (pp. 23,24)
    *1. Transporting chemicals from capillaries to neurons
    2. supporting neurons and insulating them
    3. phagocytosis — housekeeping function.*

7. Name the three types of glial cells found in the CNS and next to each,
    indicate their general function. (pp. 23-25)

    1. _astroglia_   _support cell_
    2. _microglia_   _phagocytosis_
    3. _oligodendroglia_   _myelinating function_

11

8. Explain the role of oligodendroglia in the formation of the myelin sheath. (pp. 25,26)

OBJECTIVE 2-4: Name and distinguish the function of cells in the PNS from cells in the CNS.

---

9. Indicate the function in the PNS of the following cells. Next to each, name the cell in the CNS that has similar function. (pp. 26,27)

   a. satellite cell _____   _____

   b. Schwann cell _____   _____

10. Explain how Schwann cells allow severed nerves in the PNS to regrow after injury. (p. 28)

11. Why does functional regrowth of damaged axons not occur in the CNS? (p. 28)

OBJECTIVE 2-5: Explain the function and cellular basis of the blood-brain barrier.

---

12. If trypan blue, a dye, is injected into the blood stream, the dye will appear in all tissues except the CNS. Explain why. (pp. 28,29)

13. Explain what we mean when we say that the blood-brain barrier is selectively permeable. (p. 29)

14. Name an area in the CNS where the blood-brain barrier is more permeable. (p. 29) _____

What is the adaptive significance of this more permeable barrier? (p. 29)

15. Experimental allergic encephalomyelitis resembles the disease _____. (p. 29)

What is believed to be the cause of multiple sclerosis?

Thought Questions

1. Given the discussion of regeneration of axons, why do you suppose severe injury to the head can be so serious?

2. Why is it that nearly all psychoactive drugs used to treat certain psychological disorders freely travel through the blood-brain barrier?

3

Membrane Potentials and the Transmission of Information

Essential Concepts

1. The axonal membrane is permeable only to certain molecules, such as sodium, potassium and chloride ions, and not to proteins and other large molecules. This means that normally only certain molecules can pass from the extracellular fluid outside to the intracellular fluid inside. Osmotic pressure results from the different concentrations of ions in the inside and outside of the axon. Electrostatic pressure arises from the different number of positive and negative ions in the inside and the outside of the axon. The osmotic and electrostatic forces generate the resting potential, a potential difference between the inside and the outside of the axon. This potential results from the fact that there are more positive ions in the extracellular fluid than in the intracellular fluid. The resting membrane potential is approximately -70 millivolts. The inside is negatively charged and the outside is positively charged.

2. An action potential occurs when the outside of the axonal membrane is made less positive, thereby decreasing the membrane potential. This process is called depolarization. When the membrane potential is decreased to its threshold of excitation, the outside of the axon suddenly becomes very negative, then quickly returns to normal resting potential. All this occurs in less than 2 milliseconds.

3. The action potential generated at the site of depolarization is carried down the entire length of the axon in an all-or-none fashion. The action potential does not diminish as it is transmitted along the axon. Because of this non-diminishing response, we know that the action potential is not the result of passive cable conductance of electrical charge. The depolarization caused by one action potential in a small area of the axon depolarizes the next area of the axon to threshold and another action potential is produced there. This domino effect occurs down the entire length of the axon in an undiminished fashion.

4. <u>Myelin</u> <u>sheaths</u> that surround the axonal membrane allow faster conduction of the action potential as it travels along the axon. In myelinated axons, action potentials can occur only at the <u>nodes</u> <u>of</u> <u>Ranvier</u> where there is no myelin present. The electrical disturbance of the action potential is carried by passive cable conductance to the next node and triggers an action potential there. Thus, the action potential "jumps" from node to node and is faster than the continuous conduction down an unmyelinated axon.

<u>Key Words</u>

diffusion (p. 32)

concentration gradient (p. 32)

permeable (p. 32)

osmosis (p. 33)

hydrostatic pressure (p. 34)

equilibrium (p. 34)

electrostatic pressure (p. 36)

electrolyte (p. 36)

ion (p. 36)

cation (p. 36)

anion (p. 36)

electrostatic gradient (p. 38)

Nernst equation (p. 38)

sodium-potassium pump (p. 43)

electrode (p. 45)

depolarization (p. 45)

hypopolarization (p. 45)

hyperpolarization (p. 45)

action potential (p. 47)

threshold of excitation (p. 47)

sodium carrier (p. 51)

cable properties (p. 53)

all-or-none law (p. 54)

saltatory conduction (p. 56)

epilepsy (p. 58)

LEARNING OBJECTIVES FOR CHAPTER 3

When you have mastered the material in the chapter, you will
be able to:

1. Explain how osmotic and electrostatic pressure give rise to the resting
   membrane potential of the axon.

2. Explain the use and limitation of the Nernst equation in calculating the
   membrane potential of an axon.

3. Describe the role of the sodium-potassium pump in generating the axonal
   membrane potential.

4. List and explain the ionic events that occur during an action potential.

5. Explain how an action potential is propagated along myelinated and
   unmyelinated axons.

OBJECTIVE 3-1: Explain how osmotic pressure and electrostatic pressure give rise to the resting membrane potential of
the axon.

---

1. Molecules are constantly in motion. They travel from regions of
   _____ concentration to regions of _____
   concentration. (p. 32)

2. Diffusion is characterized by movement of molecules down a
   _____. (p. 32)

3. At absolute zero (0° Kelvin), would you expect molecules to diffuse?
   Explain why or why not. (p. 32)

4. In a gravity-free situation, we pour equal volumes of a 6% sugar solution into one side of a container and a 12% sugar solution on the other
   side. Nylon mesh separates the two sides of the container. What would
   be the concentration of sugar on both sides of the container after
   several days? (p. 32)

5. What would happen if, in a gravity-free situation, equal volumes of a 20% and a 10% sugar solution were separated by a barrier that is permeable only to water? (p. 33)

    Will the volume on both sides of the barrier be the same? Why or why not? (p. 33)

6. The phenomenon described in question 5 is called osmosis. Define osmosis and explain why the situation in question 5 is an example of osmosis. (p. 33)

7. If, on earth, we pour 40 millimeters of water on one side of a semi-permeable membrane and 20 millimeters on the other side, what will the volume of water be on each side after several minutes? What kind of pressure produces these results? (pp. 34,35,36)

8. Describe the forces involved in establishing equilibrium in the following situation: on earth, we fill one side of a container divided by a semipermeable membrane with a 6% sugar solution on one side and an equal volume of a 12% sugar solution on the other. (pp. 34,35,36)

9. What are electrolytes? (p. 36) _split_
    substances that breakdown into 2 elements of opposing
    electrical charge when placed in water
    dissolved

What are the two types of ions and what electrical charge does each have? (p. 36)

cations — +

anions — −

10. What is electrostatic pressure? (p. 36)

the force exerted by the attraction or repulsion of + or −.
particles

11. Suppose we put 12 molecules of sodium acetate on one side of a membrane which is permeable to sodium but not to acetate, and 6 molecules of sodium acetate on the other side. Describe how an electrical charge would be generated by the distribution of ions. (pp. 36,37,38)

OBJECTIVE 3-2: Explain the use and limitation of the Nernst equation in calculating the membrane potential of an axon.

---

12. State the Nernst equation mathematically. Define each of the symbols. (pp. 38,39)

Now verbally state what the Nernst equation means in your own words. (p. 39)

13. What are the three assumptions of the Nernst equation? (p. 40)

    a. _____

    b. _____

    c. _____

14. Using the Nernst equation, explain, step-by-step, how -93 mV is calcu-
    lated to be the membrane potential using potassium (K^+). (p. 42)

15. Which assumption of the Nernst equation is violated by sodium (Na^+)
    and potassium (K^+) ions? (p. 42)

OBJECTIVE 3-3: Describe the role of the sodium-potassium pump in
generating the axonal membrane potential.

---

16. Cite one piece of evidence that demonstrates the existence of the
    sodium-potassium pump. (pp. 42,43)

17. Compare the permeability of the axonal membrane to sodium and potassium. (p. 43)

18. Can you explain, in terms of the Na^+-K^+ pump, why the calculated value of the membrane potential using the Nernst equation with K^+ is greater (more negative) than the empirically measured membrane potential of -70 mV? (pp. 42,43)

19. Explain why the effects of dinitrophenol and temperature changes on the sodium-potassium pump are evidence that the pump requires biochemical energy. (p. 43)

20. The outside of the axon has a _____ charge and the inside has a _____ charge. (p. 44)

OBJECTIVE 3-4: List and explain the ionic events that occur during an action potential.

---

21. What would happen to the electrical potential of a neural membrane if it were suddenly to become permeable to sodium? Why? (p. 44)

22. What are the effects, respectively, of negative and positive shocks to the outside of the giant squid axon? (p. 45)

23. Define hyperpolarization and depolarization. (p. 45)

24. What is the consequence of applying gradually stronger positive shocks to the outside of the axonal membrane? (p. 46)

How depolarized must the membrane be (in millivolts) in order for an action potential to be initiated? (p. 46) _____

25. What is meant by the following statement? "The threshold of excitation is -65 mV." (p. 47)

26. An axon is immersed in a dish of seawater containing radioactive sodium. Explain why repeated production of action potentials will lead to more and more radioactivity inside the axon but no increase in sodium concentration. (p. 47)

27. List, in proper sequence, the electrical and chemical events that comprise the action potential. (p. 48)

28. In the oscilloscope tracing shown below, indicate the ionic events responsible for each component of an action potential. Be sure to label the axes. (pp. 46-48)

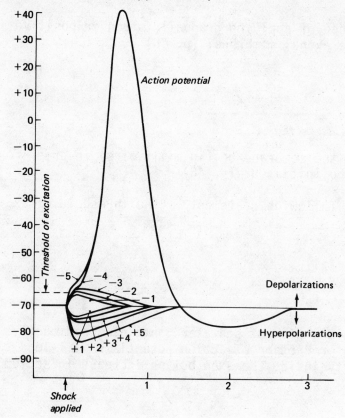

29. What two forces induce sodium ions to rush into the axon when the threshold of excitation is attained? Explain your answer. (p. 48)

30. By what means is the sodium that enters the axon during an action potential extruded following the action potential? (p. 50)

31. Contrast the short-term importance of the Na^+-K^+ pump in small and large diameter axons. Explain the differences. (p. 49)

32. Explain why the axonal membrane is less permeable to sodium ions than to potassium ions. (p. 50)

33. Why can't a temporary opening of pores in the axonal membrane explain the temporary decrease in permeability to Na^+ and K^+ during the action potential? (p. 50)

34. Describe a possible hypothesis for the transitory drop in membrane resistance to Na^+. (pp. 50,51; study Figure 3.14 on p. 51)

OBJECTIVE 3-5: Explain how an action potential is propagated along
myelinated and unmyelinated axons.

35.   If one produced a subthreshold, depolarizing shock at one end of an
axon and recorded at three locations at longer and longer distances
from the shocker, would the recorded electrical disturbance be of the
same magnitude or smaller as distance from the shocker increased?
Explain why or why not. (p. 52)

36.   What do we mean by the statement: "The transmission of subthreshold
depolarizations follows the laws describing the cable properties of
the axon"? (p. 53)

37.   What is the all-or-none law? (p. 54)

38.   Describe how myelin divides the axon into segments. (p. 56)

39. How does electrical activity generated at one node of Ranvier travel
     to the next? (pp. 56,57)

40. What is saltatory conduction? (p. 56)

41. What are the two advantages of saltatory conduction? (p. 57)

42. Explain the role of glia cells in regulating the concentration of K^+
     in the extracellular fluid. (p. 57)

43. What is thought to be the cause of epilepsy? (p. 57)

44. How do drugs that control epilepsy appear to work? (p. 57)

4

Neural Communication and the Decision-Making Process

Essential Concepts

1. The propagation of an action potential along an axon generally leads to a change in electrical potential of the postsynaptic membrane on which its terminal buttons impinge. The ionic events that compose the action potential cause synaptic vesicles filled with transmitter substance to bind to the membrane of the terminal membrane and the contents of the vesicles to be dispelled into the synaptic cleft.

2. Depending on the type of transmitter molecule released by the synaptic vesicles, the postsynaptic membrane may be either depolarized (excitatory postsynaptic potential) or hyperpolarized (inhibitory postsynaptic potential). The postsynaptic membrane integrates all the effects, both excitatory and inhibitory, of the terminal buttons synapsing on it. However, it is only the axon hillock that is capable of generating an action potential. The integrated sum of all potentials is transmitted passively to the axon hillock. If the threshold of excitation is reached at the axon hillock, an action potential will occur.

3. Transmitter substances that produce excitatory postsynaptic potentials (EPSPs) cause ionic permeability changes in the postsynaptic membrane. Sodium ions rush in and potassium ions leave the inside of the cell. Inhibitory postsynaptic potentials (IPSPs) are produced by the binding of inhibitory transmitter substance to receptor proteins embedded in the postsynaptic membrane causing potassium ions (and some chloride ions) to leave the cell. This efflux of potassium ions produces a hyperpolarization.

4. The two most common kinds of synapses are those between axons and dendrites, and axon and cell bodies; the so-called axodendritic and axosomatic synapses. Another less common type of synaptic relationship is that of the axoaxonic synapse in which an axon can reduce the amount of transmitter substance released by the terminal button of the axon onto which it synapses. This process is called presynaptic inhibition.

When you have mastered the material in the chapter, you will
be able to:

1. Describe and draw the specialized structures of the synapse.

2. Explain the processes and events involved in synaptic transmission.

3. Describe the two processes involved in terminating the postsynaptic
    potential following synaptic transmission.

4. Describe the ionic events responsible for EPSPs and IPSPs.

5. Describe the process of postsynaptic integration and explain its impor-
    tance in the transmission of information in the nervous system.

6. Describe the mechanism and importance of presynaptic inhibition.

OBJECTIVE 4-1: Describe and draw the specialized structures of the
                synapse.

---

1. Label the major structures of the synapse in the drawing below. Indicate
    the function of each structure. (pp. 60,61)

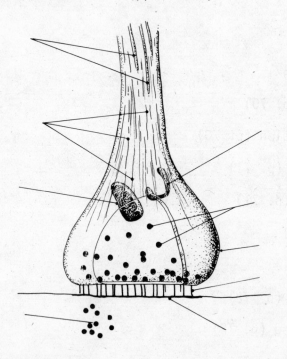

2. By what experimental procedure do we know that the presynaptic and post-synaptic membrane are attached to one another via the _____
_____? (p. 60) Include in your answer the word "synaptosome".

3. Explain how synaptic vesicles are produced within the neuron and the process by which they become located in the terminal button. (pp. 61,62)

4. What evidence suggests that protein synthesis is important for the process of receiving a message from the terminal button? (p. 62)

OBJECTIVE 4-2: Explain the processes and events involved in synaptic transmission.

5. Explain how and where transmitter substance is synthesized and packaged for use in the terminal button. (p. 62)

6. What evidence do we have that synaptic vesicles contain transmitter substance? (pp. 62,63)

7. Describe the process outlined by Heuser and Reese (1973) by which the membrane of synaptic vesicles is recycled and used again. How did they demonstrate this process? (pp. 63,64,65)

8. Explain how synaptic vesicles move to the presynaptic membrane during an action potential. (p. 65)

9. Describe the role of stenin, neurin and calcium in the release of transmitter substance into the synaptic cleft. (p. 65)

OBJECTIVE 4-3: Describe the two processes involved in terminating the postsynaptic potential following synaptic transmission.

10. What two processes restore the presynaptic membrane back to normal resting potential following the release of transmitter substance? Describe each process. (p. 66)

OBJECTIVE 4-4: Describe the ionic events responsible for EPSPs and IPSPs.

11. Differentiate between excitatory and inhibitory postsynaptic potentials. (p. 67)

12. Suppose a recording electrode is located in a postsynaptic cell while we produce action potentials by a shocker located on the presynaptic neuron. Indicate whether the recorded potentials are EPSPs or IPSPs. (p. 67, and review of Ch. 3, p. 46, if necessary)

    a. -50 mV _____

    b. -75 mV _____

    c. -90 mV _____

    d. +20 mV _____

    e.   0 mV _____

13. What is the role of receptor sites in generating the postsynaptic potential? (p. 67)

14. In order for an EPSP to occur, _____ (cations or anions?) must leak into the cytoplasm of the postsynaptic neuron. During an EPSP, sodium ions flow _____ and potassium ions flow _____ the postsynaptic neuron (pp. 68,69)

15. Explain why chloride ions do not flow into the postsynaptic cell during an EPSP. (p. 68)

16. List the ionic events that produce an IPSP. (p. 69)

```
OBJECTIVE 4-5:  Describe the process of postsynaptic integration and
                explain its importance in the transmission of infor-
                mation in the nervous system.
```

17. What is the result of delivering a hyperpolarizing shock to the outside of a squid axon just before delivering a depolarizing shock? Explain your answer. (pp. 70,71)

18. What is temporal summation? (p. 71)

    What is spatial summation? (p. 71)

19. What do neurophysiologists mean by the term "integration"? (p. 71)

20. What part of the postsynaptic neuron is capable of producing an action potential? (p. 71) _____

21. Restate in your own words the meaning of the following statement: "EPSPs and IPSPs produced at the synapses on soma and dendrites are transmitted decrementally". (p. 71)

22. What determines the rate at which a neuron fires? (p. 71)

OBJECTIVE 4-6: Describe the mechanism and importance of presynaptic inhibition.

23. Name the three kinds of synaptic relationships between neurons. (p. 72)

a. _____

b. _____

c. _____

24. Draw a diagram of an axoaxonic synapse. (p. 72)

25. What determines the amount of transmitter substance that is released during an action potential? (p. 73)

26. Explain how axoaxonic synapses work. (p. 73)

27. What might be the functional importance of axoaxonic synapses and pre-synaptic inhibition? (p. 73)

Thought Question

1. Why do you suppose cessation of EEG activity recorded from the skull is taken as medical evidence of death?

5

Biochemistry and Pharmacology of Synaptic Transmission

Essential Concepts

1. So far, at least ten <u>neurotransmitters</u> have been tentatively identified, and more are probably yet to be discovered. Several of these transmitter substances are found exclusively in the brain. The question of why there are so many neurotransmitters has several answers.

   a. Earlier evolving nervous system functions appear to have used different biochemical mechanisms than later evolving functions.

   b. The duration of the EPSP or IPSP is an important variable in the functioning of the nervous system, and the duration of the PSP depends, in part, on the type of transmitter molecule.

   c. Neural systems using different transmitter molecules allow a biochemical separation of functional systems. This separation might permit specific nervous system functions to be differentially influenced by <u>neuromodulators</u> such as <u>endogenous</u> <u>opiates</u>.

2. A variety of drugs has been discovered which can either facilitate or reduce the effectiveness of neural transmission. Facilitation of chemical transmission can occur by means of blocking the re-uptake of transmitter substance into the presynaptic terminal, by interfering with degradative presynaptic and postsynaptic enzymes and by pharmacologically inducing vesicle release. Such drugs are called <u>agonists</u>. Other drugs can reduce neural transmission by blocking the synthesis of the transmitter substance, by preventing the storage of transmitter molecules in the vesicles, by blocking the release of vesicle contents, or by blocking receptor proteins. Such drugs are called <u>antagonists</u>. Pharmacological agents have been discovered that are specific to each of the well-studied neurotransmitters.

3. <u>Acetylcholine</u> (ACh) is the excitatory transmitter substance liberated at the <u>neuromuscular junction</u>. ACh also transmits EPSPs from preganglionic to postganglionic neurons of the autonomic nervous system. In the

mammalian nervous system, there are two types of cholinergic receptors (both mediating EPSPs): muscarinic and nicotinic. The PSP produced by the release of ACh is terminated by the enzyme acetylcholinesterase.

4. Both norepinephrine and dopamine (the catecholamines) are derived from an amino acid, tyrosine. Dopamine is converted to norepinephrine by the enzyme dopamine-β-hydroxylase. Presumably, only the noradrenergic neurons synthesize this enzyme. Both the catecholamines have an inhibitory effect on neurons of the CNS. Dopamine is present exclusively in the brain. Norepinephrine, while found in the brain, is also the transmitter substance at most postganglionic terminals of the synpathetic branch of the autonomic nervous system. The PSPs produced by norepinephrine and dopamine are terminated by the re-uptake of transmitter molecules into the presynaptic terminal. Both dopamine and norepinephrine have been implicated in various forms of mental illness and several neurological disorders.

5. Serotonin (5-HT) is produced via a biosynthetic pathway starting with another amino acid, tryptophan, and has inhibitory effects on the postsynaptic membrane. Serotonin, like norepinephrine and dopamine, is found in specific, well-defined pathways of the brain.

6. Glutamic acid and gamma-amino butyric acid (GABA) are special neuronal products of the Krebs citric acid cycle and they may have been the first neurotransmitters to arise in evolution. Glutamic acid may be the principal excitatory transmitter in the brain. GABA is an inhibitory transmitter found throughout cellular areas of the brain and in certain cellular regions of the spinal cord.

7. Glycine is another amino acid neurotransmitter, which appears to have inhibitory effects in the spinal cord and possibly lower regions of the brain.

8. Other suspected neurotransmitters are taurine, aspartic acid, serine, and substance P (a polypeptide), but little is known about their location or role in the nervous system.

9. There appear to be two ways in which neurotransmitters alter the ionic permeability of the postsynaptic membrane. ACh, for example, has a relatively direct effect on receptor proteins that changes the permeability of the postsynaptic membrane. The effect of the catecholamines on the postsynaptic neuron is mediated by cyclic AMP. Cyclic AMP is a cofactor for enzymes known as kinases whose presence causes phosphorylation of membrane proteins. Phosphorylation changes the configuration of membrane proteins and leads to an increased ionic permeability of the postsynaptic membrane.

Key Words

neural inhibition (p. 77)

behavioral inhibition (p. 77)

neuromodulator (p. 78)

endogenous opiate (pp. 78,94)

agonist (p. 79)

antagonist (p. 79)

enzyme (p. 80)

false transmitter (p. 81)

acetylcholine (ACh) (p. 81)

pre- and postganglionic neurons (p. 82)

coenzyme A (p. 82)

acetylcholinesterase (AChE) (p. 83)

muscarinic receptor (p. 84)

nicotinic receptor (p. 84)

hemicholinium (p. 84)

botulinum toxin (p. 84)

atropine (p. 84)

d-tubocurarine (p. 85)

eserine (p. 85)

diisopropylfluorophosphate (DFP) (p. 85)

norepinephrine (NE) (pp. 81,86)

monoamine (p. 86)

catecholamine (p. 86)

adrenalin (p. 86)

epinephrine (p. 86)

noradrenalin (p. 86)

tyrosine (p. 86)

L-DOPA (pp. 86,90)

tyrosine hydroxylase (p. 86)

dopamine (pp. 86,87,88)

DOPA decarboxylase (p. 87)

dopamine-β-hydroxylase (p. 87)

FLA-63 (p. 87)

alpha-methyl-para-tyrosine (AMPT) (p. 87)

reserpine (p. 87)

amphetamine (p. 87)

alpha and beta receptors (p. 87)

isoproterenol (p. 87)

propranolol (p. 87)

phentolamine (p. 87)

desipramine, imipramine (pp. 87,88)

tricyclic antidepressant (p. 88)

monoamine oxidase (MAO) (p. 88)

catechol-O-methyltransferase (COMT) (p. 88)

pargyline (p. 88)

6-hydroxydopamine (6-HD) (p. 88)

deprenyl (p. 89)

gamma-hydroxybutyrate (p. 89)

apomorphine (pp. 89,90)

Parkinson's disease (p. 89)

chlorpromazine (p. 90)

5-hydroxytryptamine (5-HT) (p. 91)

serotonin (p. 91)

endorphin (p. 94)

substance P (p. 94)

oxytocin (p. 94)

histamine (p. 94)

cyclic nucleotide (p. 95)

adenyl cyclase (p. 95)

cyclic AMP (p. 96)

adenosine triphosphate (ATP) (p. 96)

kinase (p. 96)

phosphorylation (p. 96)

phosphodiesterase (p. 96)

caffeine (p. 96)

second messenger (pp. 95,96)

LEARNING OBJECTIVES FOR CHAPTER 5

When you have mastered the material in the chapter, you will
be able to:

LESSON 1: BASIC PHARMACOLOGY OF SYNAPTIC TRANSMISSION
AND THE PHARMACOLOGY OF ACETYLCHOLINE

1. Explain why there exist so many transmitter substances.

2. Describe the various ways that drugs can facilitate or impair synaptic
    transmission.

3. Describe the distribution, synthesis, deactivation and postsynaptic
    receptors of acetylcholine.

4. List the major cholinergic agonists and antagonists and describe the
    mechanism of action of each drug.

LESSON 2: PHARMACOLOGY OF THE CATECHOLAMINES, SEROTONIN,
GLUTAMIC ACID, GABA AND GLYCINE

5. Describe the distribution, synthesis and pharmacology of the catecholamines; norepinephrine and dopamine.

6. Describe the distribution, synthesis and pharmacology of serotonin.

7. Describe the pharmacology of glutamic acid, gamma-amino butyric acid
and glycine.

8. Explain the mechanisms by which neurotransmitters can produce postsynaptic activity.

LESSON 1: BASIC PHARMACOLOGY OF SYNAPTIC TRANSMISSION
AND THE PHARMACOLOGY OF ACETYLCHOLINE

OBJECTIVE 5-1: Explain why there exist so many transmitter
substances.

1. For review, what are the two possible effects that a transmitter substance can have on the postsynaptic membrane potential? (pp. 75,76)

2. Some neurotransmitters can have either an excitatory or inhibitory effect on the postsynaptic cell, depending on the nature of the
_____. (p. 76)

3. Explain why neural inhibition need not necessarily imply behavioral
inhibition. (p. 77)

4. There are three reasonable explanations for the fact that there are so
many neurotransmitters. Briefly, summarize each. (pp. 77,78,79)

5. Which two transmitter substances may have appeared first in evolution?
(p. 77)

_____

_____

6. How are GABA and glutamic acid produced? (p. 77)

7. Give two examples of neuromodulators and describe their functional role
    in the brain. (pp. 78,79)

OBJECTIVE 5-2: Describe the various ways that drugs can facilitate
or impair synaptic transmission.

---

8. Define "agonist" and "antagonist". (p. 79)

9. Describe how transmitter substance is synthesized and stored in
    vesicles within the terminal button. (p. 80)

10. What is the general function of enzymes? What is the suffix that
     denotes that a substance is an enzyme? (p. 80)

11. Explain why a drug that inactivates an enzyme important in the synthe-
     sis of a transmitter substance acts as an antagonist. (p. 80)

12. Below are listed some possible effects that drugs could have on neurons. Indicate beside each whether the drug is an agonist or an antagonist. (pp. 80,81)

a. inactivates enzyme involved in transmitter synthesis _____

b. makes vesicle membrane "leaky" _____

c. prevents release of transmitter substance _____

d. stimulates release of transmitter substance _____

e. binds to and activates postsynaptic receptors _____

f. binds to but does not activate postsynaptic receptors _____

g. deactivates enzyme involved in deactivating transmitter substance after release from terminal button _____

h. blocks re-uptake of transmitter substance _____

i. increases rate of re-uptake _____

j. inhibits cytoplasmic enzymes involved in degradation of transmitter substance _____

OBJECTIVE 5-3: Describe the distribution, synthesis, deactivation and postsynaptic receptors of acetylcholine.

---

13. Explain why the neurotransmitters acetylcholine and norepinephrine are easier to study than the other transmitter substances. (p. 81)

14. _____ is the transmitter substance liberated at neuromuscular junctions. (p. 82)

15. ACh is also an important transmitter between what two classes of cells in the autonomic nervous system? (p. 82)

16. Diagram the biochemical reaction necessary for the synthesis of ACh. (p. 82)

17. What is meant by "rate limiting" in chemical reactions? What is the rate limiting substance in the synthesis of acetylcholine? (p. 83)

18. What enzyme breaks down ACh that is released in the synaptic cleft and excess ACh within the cytoplasm? (p. 83) _____

19. Name the two types of cholinergic receptors. (p. 84)

    _____   _____

20. Where in the nervous system is each type found? (p. 84)

┌───┐
│   │
│   OBJECTIVE 5-4: List the major cholinergic agonists and antagonists │
│   and describe the mechanism of action of each drug. │
│   │
└───┘

21. What effect does hemicholinium have on cholinergic synapses? Explain how the drug works. (p. 84)

22. How is botulinum toxin produced? (p. 84)

    What action does botulinum toxin have on cholinergic synapses? (p. 84)

23. Describe the effects of black widow spider venom. (p. 84)

24. How do false transmitters work? (p. 84)

44

Give an example of a muscarinic false transmitter. (p. 84)

_____

Give an example of a nicotinic false transmitter. (pp. 84,85)

_____

25. Explain why the drug curare can be lethal. (p. 85)

26. Why is the brain not affected by curare? (p. 85)

27. What is the result of pharmacologically inhibiting the enzyme acetyl-cholinesterase? (p. 85)

Distinguish between the effects of eserine and diisopropylfluorophos-phate (DFP). (p. 85)

28. Explain why atropine is used as an antidote for organophosphate insecticide poisoning. (p. 85)

29. In the following schematic diagram of a cholinergic synapse, indicate where and how each of the following drugs works: nicotine, muscarine, hemicholinium, black widow spider venom, botulinum toxin, atropine, curare, eserine, DFP. (p. 85)

45

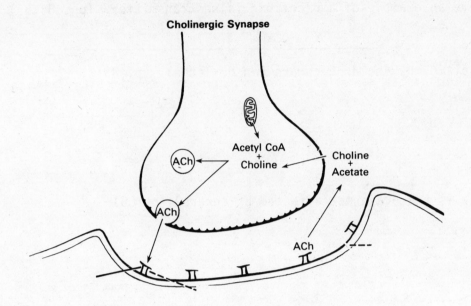

Cholinergic Synapse

ACh

Acetyl CoA
+
Choline

Choline
+
Acetate

ACh

ACh

(30.) Just to make sure you really know the major acetylcholine-related substances and their effects, match the drug on the left to the best description of its mechanism of action on the right. (pp. 84,85)

_d_ choline

_e_ botulinum toxin

_c_ atropine

_h_ d-tubocurarine

_a_ choline acetylase

_i_ black widow spider venom

_g_ eserine

_f_ DFP

_b_ hemicholinium

a. enzyme involved in ACh synthesis

b. prevents transport of choline across membrane of terminal button

c. blocks muscarinic receptors

d. rate-limiting precursor of ACh

e. prevents release of ACh

f. an irreversible inhibitor of AChE

g. short-acting (reversible) inhibitor of AChE

h. blocks nicotinic receptors

i. causes continuous release of ACh

46

> OBJECTIVE 5-5: Describe the distribution, synthesis and pharma-
> cology of the catecholamines; norepinephrine and
> dopamine.

31. Draw a schematic diagram of the autonomic nervous system showing where in the system norepinephrine and ACh are neurotransmitters (p. 83, Figure 5.2).

32. Which transmitter substances belong to the class of compounds called monoamines? (p. 86)

    Norepinephrine, dopamine, serotonin

    Which belong in the category of catecholamines? (p. 86)

    Norepinephrine and dopamine

33. What are the other common names for norepinephrine and epinephrine? (p. 86)

    _____*noradrenalin*_____   _____*adrenalin*_____

34. Where is adrenalin produced? (p. 86) _____*adrenal gland*_____

35. The liberation of NE from vesicles generally produces an *inhibitory* postsynaptic potential in the CNS. (p. 86)

36. Diagram the biosynthesis of the catecholamines. Include all relevant enzymes. (p. 87)

37. What is the effect of alpha-methyl-para-tyrosine on the synthesis of NE and dopamine? (p. 87)

inhibitory

How does AMPT work? (p. 87)

it inhibits tyrosine hydroxylase and prevents the synthesis of DOPA & thus dopamine & NE

38. Describe the effect of reserpine on noradrenergic synapses. (p. 87)

it causes the vesicular membrane to become "leaky" so that it is released and destroyed before reaching the pre synaptic membrane

What medical use does reserpine have? (p. 87)

as a hypotensive (blood pressure reducing) agent

39. Describe the actions of amphetamine on noradrenergic synapses. (p. 87)

It stimulates the release of NE and dopamine into the synaptic cleft and also retards the re-uptake of them.

(It is a potent agonist for the catecholamines

40. Just as there are two cholinergic receptors, _____*muscarinic*_____ and _____*nicotinic*_____, there are two types of adrenergic receptors, _____*alpha*_____ and _____*beta*_____. (p. 87)

41. Name some effects of pharmacological stimulation of alpha adrenergic receptors. (p. 87)

Name some effects of pharmacological stimulation of beta adrenergic receptors. (p. 87)

48

42. Indicate the effects on noradrenergic synapses of the following adrenergic drugs. (p. 87)

not effective beta

a. isoproterenol — *stimulates both alpha & beta receptors and therefore is an agonist*

b. propranolol — *Blocks Beta receptors (antagonistic)*

c. phentolamine — *Blocks Alpha receptors (antagonistic*

43. Explain why adrenergic drugs are used in treating the symptoms of asthma. (p. 87)

the relax the smooth muscles of the bronchi

44. How are the effects of NE on the postsynaptic membrane normally terminated? (p. 87)

by reuptake of the transmitter by the terminals rather than enzymatic deactivation

45. Give two examples of tricyclic antidepressant drugs. Then explain their mechanism of action. (p. 88)

pargyline — inhibits MAO which breaks down dopamine & NE thus increasing the production and liberation of monoamines

desipramine — acts as a potent inhibitor of re-uptake of NE causing the PSPs of noradrenergic synapses to be maintained longer. (Chronic depression seems to result from decreased activity in noradrenergic and/or serotonergic neurons
imipramine

46. What is the function of monoamine oxidase and catechol-O-methyltransferase? (p. 88)

47. Name a drug that liberates catecholamine stores and explain how it works. (p. 88)

48. In the schematic diagram of a noradrenergic synapse below, indicate where and how each of the following drugs works: AMPT, reserpine, FLA-63, amphetamine, pargyline, imipramine and isoproterenol. (pp. 87,88,89)

Noradrenergic Synapse

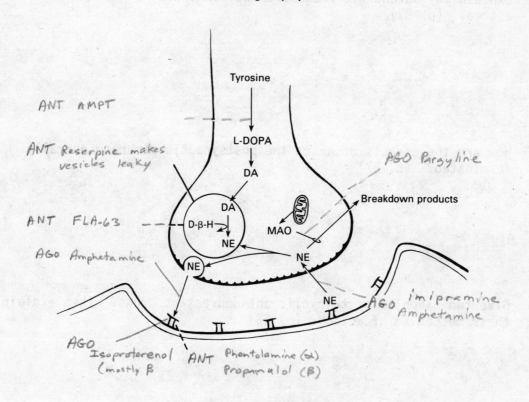

ANT AMPT

ANT Reserpine makes vesicles leaky

ANT FLA-63

AGO Amphetamine

AGO Isoproterenol (mostly β

ANT Phentolamine (α) Propranolol (β)

AGO Pargyline

AGO imipramine Amphetamine

Tyrosine

L-DOPA

DA

DA

D-β-H

NE

NE

MAO

Breakdown products

NE

NE

49. What drug selectively destroys catecholaminergic neurons? (p. 88)

Explain why this drug is selective in its effect. (p. 88)

How has this drug been useful in determining the function of catechol-aminergic pathways in the brain? (p. 88)

How must this drug be administered in order to affect noradrenergic neurons in the brain? Why? (p. 88)

50. _____ is the immediate precursor to norepi-nephrine and, therefore, its synthesis, like NE, is inhibited by _____. (p. 88)

51. Explain why deprenyl is a rather specific dopaminergic agonist. (p. 89)

52. Why is amphetamine an especially potent dopaminergic agonist? (p. 89)

It facilitates the release of the monoamines and also retards the reuptake of dopamine.

53. Some drugs selectively affect dopaminergic function without affecting noradrenergic transmission very much. Name two dopaminergic drugs and indicate their synaptic effects. (p. 89)

54. What are the symptoms of Parkinson's disease? (p. 89)

it is characterized by tremors and progressive rigidity of the limbs apparently resulting from degeneration of dopaminergic neurons in brain structures involved in movement, specifically, a pathway from the substantia nigra to the caudate nucleus.

51

What appears to be the cause of this disease? (pp. 89,90)

Explain why L-DOPA is administered to Parkinsonian patients. (p. 90)

55. Name a common antipsychotic drug and describe its effects on dopaminergic synapses. (p. 90)

Chlorpromazine by blocking dopaminergic synapses in the brain

56. What can happen when apomorphine is administered to a schizophrenic patient? Why? (p. 90)

Their symptoms return after having been brought under control by antipsychotic drugs because it directly stimulates DA receptors.

57. In the schematic diagram of a dopaminergic synapse below, indicate where and how each of the following drugs works: alpha-methyl-paratyrosine, L-DOPA, reserpine, deprenyl, amphetamine, gamma hydroxybutyrate, apomorphine and chlorpromazine. (pp. 88-90)

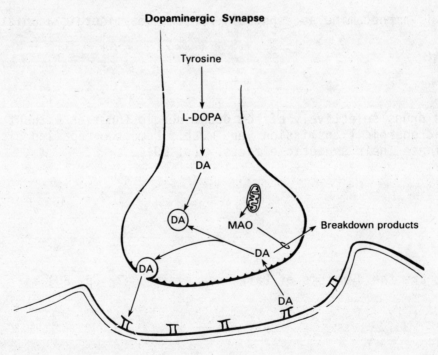

Dopaminergic Synapse

Tyrosine

L-DOPA

DA

DA

MAO

Breakdown products

DA

DA

DA

DA

58. Before we proceed to the serotonergic system, let's review the mechanism of action of the variety of catecholaminergic drugs you have been studying. Match the drug on the left to the best description of its effects on either NE or DA (or both) on the right. (pp. 86-90)

___ AMPT

___ amphetamine

___ isoproterenol

___ propranolol

___ phentolamine

___ desipramine

___ paragyline

___ 6-hydroxy-dopamine

___ reserpine

___ FLA-63

___ deprenyl

___ gamma-hydroxy-butyrate

___ apomorphine

___ chlorpromazine

a. blocks beta receptors

b. MAO inhibitor

c. stimulates release and blocks re-uptake of NE and DA

d. makes NE- and DA-containing vesicles "leaky"

e. inhibits re-uptake of NE

f. deactivates MAO type B; DA agonist

g. inhibits tyrosine hydroxylase preventing synthesis of NE and DA

h. inhibits release of dopamine

i. stimulates both alpha and beta receptors

j. antagonizes alpha receptors

k. selectively destroys catecholaminergic neurons

l. stimulates DA receptors

m. inhibitor of dopamine-β-hydroxylase

n. antipsychotic agent; blocks DA receptors

OBJECTIVE 5-6: Describe the distribution, synthesis and pharmacology of serotonin.

---

59. Diagram the biochemical pathway that leads to the production of serotonin. Include the relevant enzymes. (p. 91)

60. What is the name of the pharmacological compound that blocks the synthesis of serotonin? (p.91) _Para-chlorophenylalanine   PCPA_
    5-HT

Explain how this drug works. (p. 91)

61. What is the action of cinnanserin and methysergide on 5-HT receptors? (p. 91)

62. What is the effect of lysergic acid diethylamide (LSD) on serotonergic neurons? (p. 91)

It increases the activity neurons normally inhibited by 5-HT therefore it is a serotonergic antagonist

63. Which drug directly stimulates central 5-HT receptors? (p. 91)

quipazine

64. What pharmacological evidence suggests that serotonin, as well as norepinephrine, may play a role in clinical depression? (pp. 91,92)

Name a serotonergic antidepressive drug. (p. 91)

Amitryptyline

65. Describe the effects of iproniazid on serotonergic synapses. (p. 92)

66. Explain why the administration of 5-hydroxytryptophan can increase levels of 5-hydroxytryptamine. (p. 92)

67. Name a drug that selectively destroys 5-HT neurons. (p. 92)

_____

In what way is this drug useful in brain research? (p. 92)

68. In the schematic diagram of a serotonergic synapse below, indicate where and how each of the following drugs works: parachlorophenylala-nine, reserpine, quipazine, imipramine, iproniazid and amitryptyline. (pp. 91,92)

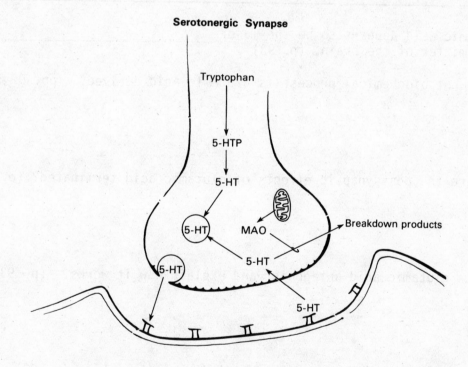

Serotonergic Synapse

Tryptophan

5-HTP

5-HT

5-HT

MAO

Breakdown products

5-HT

5-HT

5-HT

5-HT

69. Match the serotonergic drug on the left to the best description of its effects on 5-HT neurons on the right. (pp. 91,92)

___ PCPA

___ LSD

___ quipazine

___ amitryptyline

___ iproniazid

___ 5-HTP

___ 5,6-DHT

___ reserpine

a. prevents storage of 5-HT in vesicles

b. inhibits MAO; increases 5-HT levels

c. increases activity of neurons in brain that are normally inhibited by 5-HT neurons

d. precursor to 5-HT; increases 5-HT levels

e. selectively destroys 5-HT neurons

f. inhibits tryptophan hydroxylase; blocks synthesis of 5-HT

g. blocks re-uptake of 5-HT

h. stimulates 5-HT receptors

OBJECTIVE 5-7: Describe the pharmacology of glutamic acid, gamma-amino butyric acid and glycine.

---

70. Glutamic acid appears to be the major _____ transmitter of the brain. (p. 93)

71. From what biochemical process is glutamic acid derived? (pp. 92,93)

72. How are the postsynaptic effects of glutamic acid terminated? (p. 93)

73. Name a glutamic acid antagonist and explain how it works. (p. 93)

Name a glutamic acid agonist and explain how it works. (p. 93)

74. By what biochemical process is GABA produced? (p. 93)

75. What is the immediate precursor of GABA? (p. 93) _____

76. GABA generally produces _____ postsynaptic potentials
    in the gray matter of the brain. (p. 93)

77. Indicate the effects of the following pharmacological substances on GABA
    synapses. (p. 93)

    a. tetanus toxin

    b. bicuculline

    c. muscimol

    d. n-propylacetic acid

78. Why is n-propylacetic acid used to treat epilepsy? (p. 93)

79. Name three symptoms of Huntington's chorea. What is the hypothesized
    cause of this disease? (p. 93)

80. Where is glycine found in the nervous system? (p. 93)

81. What type of PSP does glycine produce? (p. 93) _____

82. Name a drug that blocks glycine receptors. (p. 94) _____
    Why is this drug considered a CNS stimulant? (p. 94)

83. Name the other suspected neurotransmitters. (p. 94)

84. Next to the transmitter substances listed below, indicate their suspected role in psychological functioning. (p. 94)

a. substance P

b. endogenous opiates

c. histamine

OBJECTIVE 5-8: Explain the mechanism by which neurotransmitters can produce postsynaptic activity.

---

85. Briefly describe how acetylcholine produces changes in the ionic permeability of postsynaptic neurons. (p. 95)

86. List or diagram the sequence of events that occurs in the postsynaptic membrane when catecholamines are liberated into the synaptic cleft. (pp. 95,96)

87. What is phosphorylation? (p. 95)

    What role might phosphorylation play in the production of the PSP?
    (p. 95)

88. Next to each molecule listed below, indicate its role in the generation
    of postsynaptic activity. (pp. 95,96)

    a. adenyl cyclase

    b. cyclic AMP

    c. ATP

    d. kinase

    e. phosphodiesterase

89. Name a phosphodiesterase inhibitor. (p. 96) _____

    Why is this drug considered to be a CNS stimulant? (p. 96)

90. Why are cyclic nucleotides often referred to as "second messengers"? (pp. 95,96)

Thought Question

1. As you know, many of the drugs that you have been learning about in this chapter have "abuse potential". In other words, there are many individuals who have become either psychologically or physiologically dependent on drugs such as morphine, amphetamine and caffeine. Can you think of a biological reason for this kind of drug dependence?

6

Introduction to the Structure of the Nervous System

Essential Concepts

1. In many ways the brain is the most protected organ of the body. Protection against physical damage is provided not only by the hard bony skull, but also by the protective layers of the meninges surrounding the CNS. The arterial blood supply to the brain originates from the vertebral and internal carotid arteries at the base of the brain. These arteries separate and join again in such a way that blood can flow along alternate routes should one branch be occluded by a blood clot. The brain is cushioned and bathed both inside and outside by cerebrospinal fluid produced by the choroid plexus in each ventricle.

2. The nervous system has two major components, the central and peripheral nervous systems. The CNS consists of the brain and spinal cord, while the cranial nerves, spinal nerves and autonomic ganglia comprise the PNS. The brain and spinal cord control the skeletal muscles and glands of the body through the spinal and cranial motor nerves. The brain and spinal cord receive information from the sense organs via the spinal and cranial sensory nerves.

3. The spinal cord distributes motor fibers to the glands and muscles of the body and collects sensory information to be transmitted upward to the brain. Fiber tracts run on the outside of the spinal cord. The inside of the spinal cord consists of cells that give rise to motor fibers (ventral horn) and cells that receive sensory information (dorsal horn).

4. The two divisions of the autonomic nervous system, the sympathetic and parasympathetic system, are concerned with the regulation of smooth muscle (e.g. the intestinal tract), cardiac muscle (heart) and glands. The sympathetic nervous system is generally concerned with the release of stored energy while the parasympathetic system usually acts to increase or conserve the body's supply of stored energy. The cell bodies of the sympathetic motor neurons are located in the intermediate horn of the gray matter of the thoracic and lumbar regions of the spinal cord. The fibers of these neurons exit via the ventral roots, but branch off

to form cholinergic synapses in the sympathetic ganglia. The axons of
the postsynaptic cells innervating target organs are usually adrenergic.
The cell bodies that give rise to the parasympathetic nerve fibers are
located in the intermediate horn of the sacral spinal cord and nuclei of
the cranial nerves residing in the brain. Unlike the sympathetic system,
parasympathetic ganglia are located very near their target organs. The
terminals of both pre- and postganglionic fibers are cholinergic.

5. The table on the following page summarizes the anatomical organization
of the brain. Next to each principal structure is a very general statement of the function of that structure or structures.

Major Division	Subdivision	Principal Structures	General Function
Forebrain	Telencephalon	cerebral cortex	- most recently evolved brain tissue - consists of 5 lobes: frontal, parietal, temporal, occipital, limbic
		basal ganglia	- amygdala, globus pallidus, caudate nucleus, putamen - concerned with motor control - major component of extrapyramidal motor system
		limbic system	- hippocampus, amygdala, septum, anterior thalamus, mammillary bodies - concerned with emotion and motivation
	Diencephalon	thalamus	- consists of relay nuclei to cerebral cortex
		hypothalamus	- control of autonomic nervous system - organizes some species-typical behavior
Midbrain	Mesencephalon	tectum	- superior colliculus (visual tectum) - inferior colliculus (auditory tectum)
		tegmentum	- reticular formation - sleep and arousal - red nucleus - part of extrapyramidal motor system - substantia nigra - part of extrapyramidal motor system - oculomotor nuclei - control of eye movements
Hindbrain	Metencephalon	cerebellum	- motor coordination
		pons	- sleep and arousal, contains some of the nuclei of the cranial nerves
	Myelencephalon	medulla oblongata	- control of vital functions: respiration, heart, muscle tonus

Key Words

vertebral column (p. 99)

neuraxis (p. 99)

anterior/posterior (p. 99)

rostral/caudal (p. 99)

dorsal/ventral (p. 99)

lateral/medial (p. 99)

superior/inferior (p. 99)

transverse section (p. 100)

coronal (or frontal) section (p. 100)

horizontal section (p. 100)

sagittal section (p. 100)

midsagittal section (p. 102)

vertebral artery (p. 103)

internal carotid artery (p. 103)

meninges (p. 104)

dura mater (p. 104)

arachnoid (p. 104)

arachnoid trabeculae (p. 105)

pia mater (p. 105)

subarachnoid space (p. 105)

cerebrospinal fluid (pp. 102, 105)

lateral ventricle (p. 107)

foramen of Monroe (p. 107)

third ventricle (p. 107)

cerebral aqueduct (p. 107)

fourth ventricle (p. 107)

choroid plexus (p. 107)

foramen of Magendie (p. 108)

foramina of Luschka (p. 108)

arachnoid granulations (p. 109)

superior sagittal sinus (p. 109)

tentorium (p. 109)

ventriculogram (p. 110)

hydrocephalus (p. 110)

forebrain (p. 110)

midbrain (p. 110)

hindbrain (p. 110)

telencephalon (p. 111)

cerebral cortex (p. 111)

basal ganglia (p. 111)

limbic system (p. 111)

sulcus (p. 111)

gyri (p. 111)

frontal lobe (p. 111)

parietal lobe (p. 111)

temporal lobe (p. 111)

occipital lobe (p. 111)

limbic lobe (p. 111)

corpus callosum (p. 111)

commissure (p. 111)

indusium griseum (p. 111)

sensory cortex (p. 114)

motor cortex (p. 114)

vagus nerve (p. 130)

cranial nerve nuclei (p. 130)

autonomic nervous system (p. 130)

sympathetic nervous system (p. 130)

parasympathetic nervous system (p. 130)

catabolism (p. 130)

spinal sympathetic ganglia (p. 132)

sympathetic chain (p. 132)

postganglionic neuron (p. 132)

anabolism (p. 132)

craniosacral system (p. 132)

LEARNING OBJECTIVES FOR CHAPTER 6

When you have mastered the material in the chapter, you will
be able to:

LESSON 1: TOPOGRAPHY, BLOOD FLOW, MENINGES AND CEREBROSPINAL FLUID

1. Label the major topographical planes of both a quadrupedal and a bipedal
    animal.

2. Describe and identify major vessels of the arterial and venous blood
    systems of the brain.

3. Describe and identify the protective meninges of the CNS.

4. Explain how cerebrospinal fluid is created and describe its flow through
    the ventricular system of the brain.

LESSON 2: FOREBRAIN, MIDBRAIN AND HINDBRAIN

5. Name and describe the major anatomical structures of the telencephalon
    and indicate the general function of each.

6. Name and describe the major anatomical structures of the diencephalon
    and indicate the general function of each.

7. Name and describe the major anatomical structures of the mesencephalon,
    metencephalon and myelencephalon and indicate the general function of
    each.

LESSON 3: THE PERIPHERAL NERVOUS SYSTEM

8. Describe the structure, subdivisions and function of the spinal cord, spinal nerves and cranial nerves.

9. Describe the anatomy and function of the sympathetic and parasympathetic divisions of the autonomic nervous system.

LESSON 1: TOPOGRAPHY, BLOOD FLOW, MENINGES AND CEREBROSPINAL FLUID

OBJECTIVE 6-1: Label the major topographical planes of both a quadrupedal and a bipedal animal.

---

1. What structures compose the central nervous system (CNS)? (p. 99)

What structures compose the peripheral nervous system (PNS)? (p. 99)

2. In the sketches below of a four-legged animal and a human, label the anterior, posterior, rostral, caudal, dorsal, ventral, medial and lateral surfaces. (pp. 99,100)

3. In the diagrams below of the nervous system of an alligator and human, label the following planes: transverse, coronal, sagittal, horizontal and midsagittal. (pp. 100,101)

CNS of Alligator   **CNS of Human**

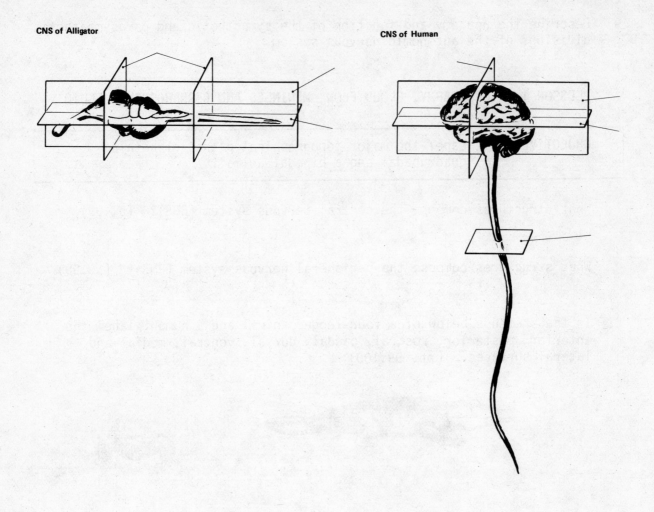

OBJECTIVE 6-2: Describe and identify the major vessels of the arterial and venous blood systems of the brain.

4. Support, with facts, the claim that the brain is the most protected organ of the body. (p. 102)

70

5. How does the brain differ from the rest of the body with regard to the constancy of its blood supply? (p. 102)

The brain receives a constant 20% of the blood flow from the heart where other parts receive according to need.

Why does the brain require a consistent blood supply? (p. 102)

because it can not store its fuel or extract energy without oxygen like the muscles can.

6. Explain how regional blood flow is controlled by smooth muscle in the walls of arterioles. (p. 102)

7. An increased rate of metabolism produces excess _____.
(p. 102)

How do blood vessels of the brain change in response to excess CO_2?
(pp. 102,103)

8. Name the two major arteries serving the brain, and indicate which part of the brain each serves. (p. 103)

_____

_____

9. What is the adaptive significance of the joining and separating of the major arteries at the base of the brain? (p. 104)

If there is a blockage in one artery, the supply of blood has an alternate pathway so that no area of the brain will be without a supply of blood

10. The drawing on the following page depicts a ventral view of the human brain. Label the vertebral, basilar, internal carotid and middle cerebral arteries. (p. 104)

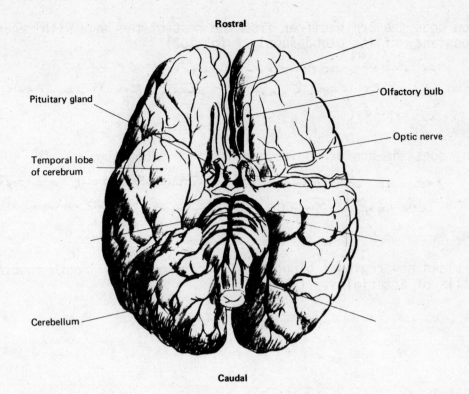

Rostral

Pituitary gland

Temporal lobe
of cerebrum

Cerebellum

Olfactory bulb

Optic nerve

Caudal

11. Draw a schematic diagram of a lateral view of the venous system of the brain. Label the middle cerebral vein, superior sagittal sinus, internal cerebral vein and the internal jugular vein. (p. 105)

72

```
┌─────────────────────────────────────────────────────────────────┐
│  OBJECTIVE 6-3:  Describe and identify the protective meninges of │
│                  the CNS.                                         │
└─────────────────────────────────────────────────────────────────┘
```

12. Describe the three layers of the meninges from the outer surface to
    the inner layer. (pp. 104,105)

    dura mater
    arachnoid
    pia mater .

13. Through which part of the meninges do large blood vessels flow? (p. 105)

```
┌─────────────────────────────────────────────────────────────────┐
│  OBJECTIVE 6-4:  Explain how cerebrospinal fluid is created and   │
│                  describe its flow through the ventricular system │
│                  of the brain.                                    │
└─────────────────────────────────────────────────────────────────┘
```

14. Indicate two ways in which cerebrospinal fluid protects the brain.
    (p. 107)

15. Where is cerebrospinal fluid manufactured in the brain? Be specific.
    (p. 107) *In the three ventricles by choroid plexus*

16. Describe the production, circulation and reabsorption of cerebrospinal
    fluid. (pp. 107,108,109)

17. Describe the flow of CSF through the lateral ventricle, foramen of Monroe, third ventricle, cerebral aqueduct, fourth ventricle and central canal. (p. 108)

18. What is the cause of the "punch-drunk" syndrome of seasoned prize fighters? (pp. 109,110)

19. Explain how a brain tumor can often be detected by a ventriculogram. (p. 110)

20. What is the cause of hydrocephalus? (p. 110)

The body's inability to reabsorb cerebrospinal fluid.

By what method can a neurologist detect this condition? (p. 110)

by looking into the eye.

LESSON 2: FOREBRAIN, MIDBRAIN AND HINDBRAIN

> OBJECTIVE 6-5: Name and describe the major anatomical structures of the telencephalon and indicate the general function of each.

21. What structures constitute the telencephalon? (p. 111)

22. Distinguish between a sulcus and a gyrus. (p. 111)

23. Explain why highly evolved mammals possess many gyri and sulci. (p. 111)

24. What is the function of the corpus callosum? (p. 111)

25. In the space provided on the following page, draw a diagram of both the lateral and medial surfaces of the brain. Label the lobes. Indicate the location of motor cortex, visual cortex, auditory cortex, somatosensory cortex and Broca's speech area. (pp. 111-114)

26. What structures comprise the limbic system? Indicate their relative
    locations on a schematic diagram in the space provided on the follow-
    ing page. (pp. 114,115; Figure 6.13).

27. What structures compose the basal ganglia? (p. 115)

amygdala, globus pallidus, caudate nucleus, and putamen

The basal ganglia are concerned with motor control and compose a major portion of the _*extrapyramidal motor*_ system. (p. 115)

OBJECTIVE 6-6: Name and describe the major anatomical structures of the diencephalon and indicate the general function of each.

---

28. What two structures make up the diencephalon? (p. 117)

*thalamus*   _*hypothalamus*_

29. From what structure does neocortex receive most of its neural input? (p. 117) _*the thalamus*_

30. Define: thalamic sensory relay nuclei. (p. 118)

Name three thalamic sensory relay nuclei and indicate to what regions of cortex the axons of each nucleus project. (p. 118)

a. _____ → _____

b. _____ → _____

c. _____ → _____

31. Indicate where each of the following thalamic nuclei project their axons. (p. 118)

a. ventrolateral nucleus →

b. dorsomedial nucleus →

c. pulvinar →

d. anterior nucleus →

32. In relation to the thalamus, where is the hypothalamus located? (p. 120) _____

Specify the major functions of the hypothalamus. (pp. 120,121)

OBJECTIVE 6-7: Name and describe the major anatomical structures of the mesencephalon, metencephalon and myelencephalon, and indicate the general function of each.

---

33. What are the two major divisions of the midbrain? (p. 121)

34. What structures comprise the tectum? (p. 121)

What structures comprise the tegmentum? (p. 122)

35. In what sensory functions are the superior and inferior colliculi involved? (pp. 121,122)

36. What is meant by the statement that mammals have "two visual systems"? (p. 122)

37. Generally describe the structure and function of the reticular formation. (p. 122)

38. Name the two components of the metencephalon. (pp. 111,122,123,124)

   _____

   _____

39. What are the major functions of the cerebellum? (p. 122)

   What is the effect of cerebellar damage on motor movements? (p. 123)

40. In the schematic representation of the human brainstem shown on the following page, label the cerebral peduncles, pons, medulla and the structures already mentioned. (p. 123)

40.

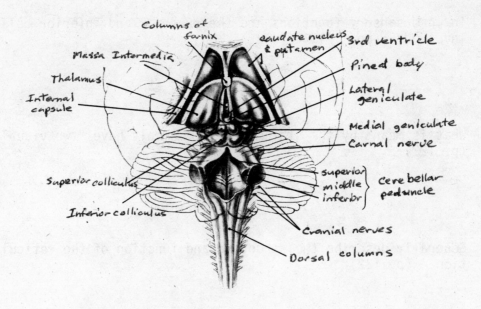

Columns of fornix · Massa Intermedia · Thalamus · Internal capsule · caudate nucleus & putamen · 3rd ventricle · Pineal body · Lateral geniculate · Medial geniculate · Carnal nerve · Superior colliculus · Inferior colliculus · superior middle inferior · Cerebellar peduncle · Cranial nerves · Dorsal columns

41. What are the functions of the medulla? (p. 124)

LESSON 3: THE PERIPHERAL NERVOUS SYSTEM

> OBJECTIVE 6-8: Describe the structure, subdivisions and function of
> the spinal cord, spinal nerves and cranial nerves.

42. What are the two principal functions of the spinal cord? (p. 124)

43. The spinal cord is covered by a bony protection called the
_____. (p. 124)

44. Name the four regions of the spinal cord, from rostral to caudal.
(p. 124)

a. ___cervical_____

b. ___thoracic_____

c. ___lumbar_____

d. ___sacral_____

80

45. Describe the anesthetic procedure sometimes used in childbirth. (p. 124)

46. Describe how the thirty-one pairs of spinal nerves emerge from the spinal cord and vertebral columns. (p. 124)

47. Unlike the brain, the spinal cord's white matter is on the _____ and the gray matter is located on the _____. (p. 125)

48. Where are the cell bodies that give rise to axons afferent to the spinal cord located? Are they considered inside or outside the CNS? (p. 128)

49. Where do the cell bodies that give rise to ventral roots reside? (p. 128)

50. In the space provided on the following page, draw cross-section through the vertebral column and spinal cord showing the following: topographical planes, afferent sensory nerve, efferent motor nerve, dorsal root ganglion, ventral horn, spinal nerve, gray matter, white matter, vertebral column and meninges. (p. 128)

51. In the space below, draw a schematic diagram of the base of the brain, indicating the location and function of the twelve cranial nerves. (pp. 129,130)

```
┌─────────────────────────────────────────────────────────────────────┐
│       OBJECTIVE 6-9:  Describe the anatomy and functions of the sympa-│
│                       thetic and parasympathetic divisions of the auto-│
│                       nomic nervous system.                           │
└─────────────────────────────────────────────────────────────────────┘
```

52. What are the three kinds of tissue that are regulated by the autonomic nervous system? (p. 130)

    a. _____smooth muscle_____

    b. _____cardiac muscle_____

    c. _____glands_____

53. Name the two subdivisions of the ANS.   (pp. 130-132)

    _____sympathetic_____   _____para sympathetic_____

Make a general statement of the function of each division. (pp. 130-132)

54. Give several examples of the effects of activating the sympathetic nervous system. (pp. 130-132)

55. The cell bodies of the sympathetic motor neurons are located in the _____intermediate_____ horn of the gray matter of which two regions of the spinal column? (p. 132)

    a. _____thoracic region_____

    b. _____lumbar region_____

56. All synapses within the sympathetic ganglia use _____cholinergic_____ as their transmitter substance. The terminal endings on target organs of the sympathetic division of the ANS use _____noradrenergic_____ as their transmitter substance, except for _____sweet_____ glands, which use _____. (p. 132)

57. Give several examples of parasympathetic ANS activity. (p. 132)

58. Why is the parasympathetic system often referred to as the craniosacral system? (p. 132)

59. How does the location of parasympathetic ganglia differ from the location of sympathetic ganglia? (p. 132)

60. Draw a diagram showing the relationship between the spinal cord and the sympathetic ganglia. Label the intermediate horn, the dorsal and ventral root, white and gray ramus, sympathetic chain and spinal nerves. Also, indicate the neurotransmitters at each synapse. (p. 131)

61. In what two regions of the CNS are the cell bodies that give rise to preganglionic parasympathetic nerve fibers located? (p. 132)

62. What neurotransmitter is used by pre- and postganglionic neurons in the parasympathetic system? (pp. 131,132)

_____

63. Indicate which division of the autonomic nervous system is responsible for each of the following physiological responses. (pp. 130-134)

a. digestive processes _____

b. increased heart rate _____

c. dilation of pupils _____

d. increased respiration _____

e. penile erection _____

f. sweating _____

g. salivation _____

h. secretion of adrenalin _____

7

Research Methods of Physiological Psychology

afferent – inward
efferent – outward

Essential Concepts

1. One of the first steps in understanding the nervous system is the deter-
    mination of neuroanatomical connections among brain structures. A com-
    plete structural description of the brain requires that we know both the
    afferents to and the efferents from each nucleus in each division of the
    brain. The Nauta-Gygax histological procedure selectively stains degen-
    erating axons following destruction by a brain lesion of the cell bodies
    of those fibers (anterograde degeneration). This method, as well as
    amino acid autoradiography, specifies the efferents of a given brain
    structure. The horseradish peroxidase method can tell us from what
    other regions a given area of the brain receives its afferent fibers.
    The afferents of a given nucleus or region of the brain can also be
    known by recording the electrical activity of that area while electric-
    ally stimulating elsewhere in the brain. The stereotaxic apparatus and
    atlas are used when lesioning, stimulating or recording from structures
    below the surface of the brain.

2. The recent development of the CAT scan and positron emission transverse
    tomography has permitted the study of the living brain without danger-
    ous surgical procedures. These techniques are valuable in the medical
    diagnosis and location of brain tumors, lesions and other abnormalities.

3. Lesioning, stimulation and recording techniques are also used to deter-
    mine the function of various brain structures. By observing systematic
    changes or deficits in behavior of an experimental animal after the
    destruction of a given structure, we can make inferences about the func-
    tion of that structure in the intact animal. Likewise, by observing
    consistent changes in the animal's behavior when the brain is stimulated
    in a defined area, we can conclude that the structure plays a role in
    the behavior we observe. The conclusions drawn from the results ob-
    tained with both techniques must be made with care and some complica-
    tions in interpretation are discussed in the text.

4. It is possible to record the electrical activity of large populations of neurons with a <u>macroelectrode</u> or of single neurons with <u>microelectrodes</u>. The summed activity of millions of cells may be recorded when a **sensory** stimulus is presented to the human or animal subject. Such electrical activity evoked by a visual stimulus is referred to as a visual <u>evoked potential</u>. "Spontaneous" electrical activity recorded from the surface of the brain or scalp and displayed on an oscilloscope or ink-writing oscillograph is referred to as an <u>electroencephalogram</u>. This technique has been used extensively in the diagnosing of epilepsy and brain tumors.

5. Pathways of neurons that use the same monoamine neurotransmitter have been discovered using the <u>histofluorescence</u> technique. Monoamines such as norepinephrine, dopamine and serotonin fluoresce when exposed to formaldehyde gas. Furthermore, the sensitivity of single neurons to a variety of neurotransmitters can be determined using <u>double-barrelled micropipettes</u>. Minute amounts of transmitter substance are <u>iontophoretically</u> applied onto the surface of a neuron or inside the cell body while recording the evoked electrical activity through the second barrel of the micropipette.

6. The role of neurotransmitters in the organization of behavior can be studied by administering drugs which inhibit the production, release or re-uptake of a given transmitter substance and observing the behavioral effect of stimulation or inhibition of the synapses that use that neurotransmitter. More specific information can be obtained by injecting drugs or neurotransmitters directly into the brain through a small <u>cannula</u> placed under stereotaxic guidance.

7. The <u>radioactive labelling</u> of hormones and other behaviorally relevant molecules has proven to be an extremely valuable technique in determining the areas of the nervous system that are particularly sensitive to these molecules. The molecule of interest is labelled with a radioactive tracer then administered to the animal intravenously. <u>Autoradiography</u> allows the radioactive molecules to be "seen" in different regions of the brain. The distribution of radioactivity specifies the brain structures that have a selective affinity for the hormone.

<u>Key Words</u>

autolytic enzyme (p. 138)

fixative (p. 138)

formalin (p. 138)

perfusion (p. 138)

rotary microtome (pp. 139,140)

sliding microtome (pp. 139,140)

embedding material (p. 140)

paraffin (p. 140)

nitrocellulose (pp. 140,141)

albumin (p. 141)

histological stain (p. 142)

Nissl substance (p. 142)

cresyl violet (p. 142)

myelin stain (p. 143)

hematoxylin (p. 143)

Golgi-Cox stain (p. 143)

Nauta-Gygax stain (p. 144)

anterograde degeneration (p. 145)

amino acid autoradiography (p. 146)

horseradish peroxidase (p. 147)

computerized axial tomography (CAT Scan) (p. 149)

positron emission transverse tomography (PETT) (p. 150)

stereotaxic apparatus (p. 151)

stereotaxic atlas (p. 151)

bregma (p. 152)

aspiration (p. 156)

cautery (p. 156)

d.c. lesion (p. 156)

radiofrequency lesion (p. 156)

chronic electrode (p. 157)

microelectrode (p. 158)

single-unit recording (p. 158)

macroelectrode (p. 158)

micropipette (p. 158)

amplifier (p. 159)

filtration (p. 159)

output device (p. 160)

oscilloscope (p. 160)

evoked potential (p. 162)

ink-writing oscillograph (p. 162)

electroencephalogram (EEG) (p. 163)

analog (p. 163)

digital (p. 163)

latency (p. 165)

focal epilepsy (p. 166)

aura (p. 166)

double-barreled micropipette (p. 169)

cannula (p. 171)

radioactive tracer (p. 171)

LEARNING OBJECTIVES FOR CHAPTER 7

When you have mastered the material in the chapter, you will
be able to:

LESSON 1: HISTOLOGY AND MEDICAL PROCEDURES FOR STUDY OF THE LIVING BRAIN

1. Describe the steps involved and the rationale for the following neuroanatomical procedures: perfusion, fixation, sectioning and staining.

2. Describe the techniques involved in the following histological stains
and explain what kind of information each stain yields to the physiological psychologist: cresyl violet, hemotoxylin, Golgi-Cox, Nauta-
Gygax, amino acid autoradiography and horseradish peroxidase.

3. Describe the procedures involved, the logic underlying and the information yielded by computerized axial tomography and positron emission
transverse tomography.

LESSON 2: STEREOTAXIC SURGERY, CHEMICAL AND ELECTRICAL
STIMULATION AND RECORDING TECHNIQUES

4. Describe all the steps involved in stereotaxic surgery.

5. Describe how brain lesions are surgically created and explain the uses
of brain lesion techniques in studying the nervous system.

6. Describe the rationale and procedures of the following methods of recording the brain's electrical activity: single-unit recording, multi-
unit recording, EEG recording and evoked potential recording.

7. Describe the rationale for and procedures involved in electrical stimulation of the brain.

8. Describe the procedures involved in and the uses of the following chemical techniques: histofluorescence, psychopharmacology, iontophoresis
and radioactive tracing.

LESSON 1: HISTOLOGY AND MEDICAL PROCEDURES FOR STUDY OF THE LIVING BRAIN

OBJECTIVE 7-1: Describe the steps involved in and the rationale for
the following neuroanatomical procedures: perfusion,
fixation, sectioning and staining.

---

1. Following is a typical list of the steps, in proper order, that the
neuroanatomist uses in studying the structure of the nervous system.
Next to each, briefly indicate the rationale for and the procedures
involved. (pp. 138-142)

a. perfusion

b. remove intact brain from skull

c. fix tissue in formalin

d. soak brain in sucrose

e. section brain on freezing microtome

f. stain section

2. What are the two most commonly used embedding substances? (pp. 140,141)

_____   _____

3. Why is a microscope slide usually coated with albumin before mounting
sections of neural tissue onto the slide? (p. 141)

4. Describe the ratioanale for and the procedures involved in the most fre-
quently used cell-body stain, cresyl violet. (pp. 142,143)

5. What aspect of brain cells is stained by hematoxylin and for what purpose is this stain used? (p. 143)

6. Explain how the Golgi-Cox stain works and what information about brain
cells is revealed by this histological procedure. (pp. 143,144)

7. Name an example of a degenerating-axon stain and explain how it works
and why it is used. (pp. 144,145)

8. Explain in a diagram the process of anterograde degeneration. (p. 145)

9. List the steps involved in amino acid autoradiography. (pp. 146-147)

10. Explain the rationale that underlies this technique and what information is revealed about neural circuitry. (p. 147)

11. Explain how horseradish peroxidase is used to study neural circuitry. (p. 147)

12. Contrast the information yielded by the HRP technique with that yielded by autoradiography. (pp. 147,148)

OBJECTIVE 7-3: Describe the procedures involved, the logic underlying and the information yielded by computerized axial tomography and positron emission transverse tomography.

13. Explain, in detail, how a CAT scan works. (p. 149)

14. What are the medical benefits of this new technique? (p. 149)

15. Explain how positron emission transverse tomography works and what information about the living brain this technique yields. (p. 150)

LESSON 2: STEREOTAXIC SURGERY, CHEMICAL AND ELECTRICAL
STIMULATION AND RECORDING TECHNIQUES

OBJECTIVE 7-4: Describe all the steps involved in stereotaxic
surgery.

16. Explain how bone sutures on the surface of the skull, such as bregma, are used in stereotaxic brain surgery. (pp. 151,152)

17. Explain how a stereotaxic atlas is used in stereotaxic surgery. (pp. 151-153)

18. List, in order, the steps involved in the use of the stereotaxic apparatus and stereotaxic coordinates in brain surgery. (pp. 153,154)

a. _____

b. _____

c. _____

d. _____

e. _____

19. What three measurements, taken relative to bregma, do we need in order to place an electrode into a subcortical brain structure? (p. 153)

OBJECTIVE 7-5: Describe how brain lesions are surgically created and explain the uses of brain lesion techniques in studying the nervous system.

---

20. What is the rationale for using the brain lesion technique in determining the function of a brain structure? (p. 155)

21. Give three reasons why we must be careful when we interpret the information gathered concerning the function of a brain structure by the use of the lesion technique. (p. 155)

22. What role does histological evaluation play in experimental stereotaxic surgery and brain lesion/behavioral studies? (p. 155)

23. There are five procedures commonly used to make brain lesions. They are aspiration, cauterization, d.c. lesioning, radiofrequency lesioning and specific neurochemical lesioning. Describe each and note the difficulties and/or advantages of each. (pp. 156,157)

a. aspiration

b. cauterization

c. d.c. lesions

d. radiofrequency lesions

e. neurochemical lesions

OBJECTIVE 7-6: Describe the rationale and procedures of the following methods of recording the brain's electrical activity: single-unit recording, multiunit recording, EEG recording and evoked potential recording.

24. Differentiate between acute and chronic electrical recording. (p. 157)

25. Describe the use of microelectrodes. (p. 158)

26. How is a metal microelectrode made? (p. 158)

27. Explain how glass microelectrodes work. (p. 158)

28. Differentiate between macroelectrodes and microelectrodes. (pp. 158,159)

29. Explain why amplifiers are used to filter and amplify electrical signals recorded from the brain. (p. 159)

30. Explain why output devices are needed in electrophysiological experiments. Give two examples of commonly used output devices. (p. 160)

31. In the space provided on the following page, diagram and explain how an oscilloscope works. (p. 160)

32. Which axis of an oscilloscopic trace usually indicates time? (p. 160)

    _____

33. Which deflection plates inside the oscilloscope are responsible for the
    time dimension? (p. 160)

    _____

34. Describe the use of a loudspeaker in recording from single units, say,
    in the visual cortex of a cat. (p. 161)

35. What does an evoked potential represent? (p. 162)

36. Explain how ink-writing oscillographs (or polygraphs) are used to re-
    cord the electroencephalogram. (pp. 162,163)

37. Explain what we mean when we say that a computer can convert an analog signal to a digital signal. (pp. 163,164)

38. What is the reason for averaging evoked potentials? (p. 165)

39. What is a possible problem in interpreting averaged evoked potentials? (p. 165)

40. Explain what information the combination of behavioral study and electrical recording experiments can yield to the physiological psychologist. (pp. 165,166)

OBJECTIVE 7-7: Describe the rationale for and procedures involved in electrical stimulation of the brain.

41. Explain how electrical stimulation can be used to determine neuroanatomical interconnections. (p. 166)

42. Below is a schematic representation of the means by which one area of
    the brain can be stimulated while recording in another area. Using
    the diagram, explain, step by step, how this technique works.
    (pp. 166,167)

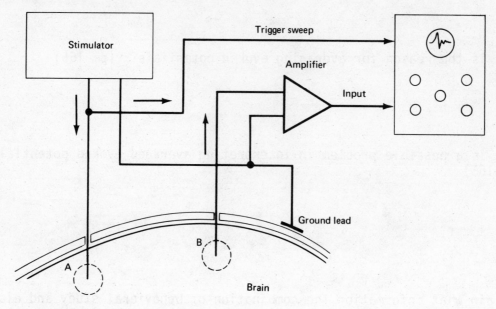

43. Explain how ablation of relatively small areas of brain tissue can help
    prevent the seizures and convulsions of focal epilepsy. (p. 166)

44. Describe Wilder Penfield's technique for determining the site of an
    epileptic focus in the brains of his patients. (p. 167)

45. Explain what electrical brain stimulation in behaving animals can tell us about brain function. (p. 168)

46. What are two problems inherent in the interpretation of the results from such behavioral studies? (pp. 168,169)

OBJECTIVE 7-8: Describe the procedures involved in and uses of the following chemical techniques: histofluorescence, psychopharmacology, iontophoresis and radioactive tracing.

---

47. Describe the use of the histofluorescence technique in tracing mono-amine pathways in the brain. (p. 169)

48. Describe the use of a double-barreled micropipette in determining the effective neurotransmitter for a single neuron. (pp. 169,170)

49. What inferences can be drawn from observing the effects of neurotransmitter inhibitors on behavior? Give an example. (pp. 170,171)

50. Describe a technique whereby a small area of the brain can be directly inhibited or excited chemically. (p. 171)

51. Describe how one can determine the rate at which proteins are produced in a given brain nucleus. (p. 171)

52. What is estrogen? (p. 171)

What technique would you employ to determine the brain structures into which estrogen is taken up? (pp. 171,172)

_____

Describe the rationale behind this technique. (p. 172)

53. What are the functional inferences which can be drawn from autoradiography experiments like these? (p. 172)

What is a potential problem with this method?

Integrative Questions

1. As you know, the lateral geniculate nucleus (LGN) of the thalamus is a specific thalamic relay nucleus of the visual system. However, there was a time not too many years ago that this fact was unknown. Given all the modern techniques at your disposal, how would you determine that the LGN is an important thalamic relay nucleus necessary for complex visual pattern recognition?

2. Many women report changes in their emotional state as a function of their menstrual cycle. This suggests that sex hormones play a role in our mood state. How would you determine which hormones and which brain structures might be involved in cyclic hormonal influences on mood? For ethical reasons, nonhuman subjects would be necessary for many experiments involved in answering this type of question.

3. The transmitter substance, dopamine, has been implicated in Parkinson's disease. What experiments would you perform to discover a) which dopamine cells are involved, and b) what might be the best pharmacological treatment?

4. Damage to the hippocampus, a major structure of the limbic system, can result in serious memory impairments in humans. Describe some experimental procedures that might tell us more precisely the role of the hippocampus in memory.

8

Receptor Organs and the Transduction of Sensory Information

Essential Concepts

1. In order for the world to affect our behavior, physical energy must be transduced into neural energy. Stimulus transduction is the function of sensory receptor cells. Some receptors are capable of generating an action potential when stimulus intensity is great enough. Other sensory cells do not have axons but are capable of producing slow potentials or receptor potentials that are transmitted to other neurons that, in turn, produce action potentials.

2. There are two classes of photoreceptors, rods and cones. Rods contain the photopigment rhodopsin, which consists of two parts, opsin and retinal. When rhodopsin is exposed to photons, it breaks up into its constituent molecules. This fission results in changes in the permeability of the rod membrane. The receptor potential produced in the rod travels through the various retinal cells and produces an action potential in the ganglion cell. It is the axons of these cells that make up the optic nerve.

3. Sound waves strike the tympanic membrane whose movement vibrates the ossicles of the middle ear. The movement of these bones on the oval window sets the fluid of the cochlea into vibration, thus bending the basilar membrane. This physical distortion of the basilar membrane produces a shearing force on the cilia of the auditory hair cells, producing a receptor potential that alters the flow of transmitter substance to dendrites of afferent neurons of the cochlear nerve.

4. The vestibular system has two components. The vestibular sacs respond to the force of gravity and inform the brain about the head's position. The semicircular canals respond to changes in the rotation of the head. The crista residing in the semicircular canals contain hair cells. Angular acceleration of the head causes the endolymph inside the canal to flow over the crista, exerting a shearing force on the cilia of the hair cells. The receptive tissue of the vestibular sacs also contains hair cells, the cilia of which are embedded in a gelatinous mass containing

otoconia. As the orientation of the head changes the weight of the oto-conia produces a shearing force on the cilia of hair cells.

5. Cutaneous sensation may be divided into three broad categories -- pressure, temperature and pain. The skin is innervated by both free nerve endings and axons that terminate in specialized organs (Pacinian corpuscles, Meissner's corpuscles, Merkel's disks, Iggo corpuscles and Krause end bulbs). Pressure appears to be transduced by both free nerve endings and encapsulated receptors. Pain appears to be transduced by free nerve endings that produce receptor potentials when exposed to extracellular substances associated with tissue damage.

6. We are aware of the position and movements of limbs and the distention of viscera through the activity of kinesthetic and organic afferent fibers to the CNS, respectively. Sensory endings on intrafusal muscle fibers signal muscle length. Golgi tendon organs respond to tension exerted by the muscle on the tendon. Pacinian corpuscles located in the fascia of muscles detect pressure and free nerve endings signal the pain that results from prolonged contraction of muscles. Pacinian corpuscles and free nerve endings are also found in the outer layers of many internal organs and give rise to organic sensations of deep pressure and pain. Somatosensory fibers enter the CNS via cranial and spinal nerves. Organic sensitivity is conveyed over fibers that travel with efferents of the ANS.

7. Taste receptor cells are not neurons, but are specialized cells that synapse with dendrites of sensory neurons. There are only four qualities of taste: bitter, sour, sweet and salty. Substances that are tasted possess some molecular characteristics that are recognized by the taste cell receptors. This molecular recognition changes the permeability of the cell and produces a receptor potential. Taste buds synapse with fibers of the facial, glossopharyngeal and vagus nerves.

8. Olfactory receptors, embedded in the olfactory epithelium , possess cilia. Odor molecules change the permeability of cilia and the potential is propagated down the cell body and finally to the axon where generator potentials are translated into altered rates of firing. Axons of olfactory receptors synapse with dendrites of mitral cells in the olfactory bulbs. The axons of mitral cells form the olfactory nerve.

Key Words

sensory transduction (p. 174)

generator potential (p. 175

receptor potential (p. 175)

somatosenses (p. 175)

VISION:

sclera (p. 177)

conjunctive (p. 177)

cornea (p. 177)

iris (p. 177)

ciliary muscle (p. 177)

retina (p. 177)

posterior chamber (p. 177)

rod (p. 177)

cone (p. 177)

fovea (p. 178)

optic disk (p. 178)

blind spot (p. 178)

photoreceptive layer (p. 179)

bipolar cell layer (p. 179)

ganglion cell layer (p. 179)

photoreceptor lamella (p. 179)

photon (p. 180)

photopigment (p. 181)

opsin (p. 181)

retinal (p. 181)

retinol (p. 181)

rhodopsin (p. 181)

all-trans-retinal (p. 182)

11-cis-retinal (p. 182)

bipolar cell (p. 185)

horizontal cell (p. 185)

amacrine cell (p. 185)

ganglion cell (p. 185)

AUDITION:

pinna (p. 188)

external auditory canal (p. 188)

tympanic membrane (p. 188)

tensor tympani (p. 189)

ossicle (p. 189)

malleus, incus and stapes (p. 189)

oval window (p. 189)

stapedius muscle (p. 189)

cochlea (p. 189)

hair cell (p. 189)

Deiters' cell (p. 189)

basilar membrane (p. 189)

reticular membrane (p. 189)

tectorial membrane (p. 189)

organ of Corti (p. 189)

round window (p. 189)

scala vestibuli (p. 189)

scala tympani (p. 190)

cuticular plate (p. 193)

cochlear nerve (p. 193)

cochlear microphonic (p. 193)

perilymph (p. 193)

endolymph (p. 193)

cortilymph (p. 193)

spiral ganglion (p. 195)

superior olivary nucleus (p. 197)

VESTIBULAR SYSTEM:

vestibular sac (p. 197)

semicircular canal (p. 197)

utricle (p. 198)

saccule (p. 198)

ampulla (p. 198)

crista (p. 198)

cupula (p. 199)

otoconia (p. 200)

kinocilium (p. 201)

stereocilia (p. 201)

vestibular nerve (p. 201)

vestibular ganglion (p. 202)

fastigial nucleus (p. 202)

vestibular nucleus (p. 202)

SKIN SENSES:

mechanoreceptor (p. 203)

nocioreceptor (p. 203)

glabrous skin (p. 203)

Iggo corpuscle (p. 204)

Pacinian corpuscle (p. 204)

Meissner's corpuscle (p. 205)

Merkel's disk (p. 205)

Krause end bulb (p. 205)

mucocutaneous zone (p. 205)

kinesthesia (p. 209)

intrafusal muscle fiber (p. 209)

Golgi tendon organ (p. 209)

GUSTATION:

anosmia (p. 211)

taste bud (p. 211)

papilla (p. 211)

chorda tympani (p. 213)

OLFACTION:

olfactory epithelium (p. 215)

olfactory bulb (p. 215)

cribiform plate (p. 215)

mitral cell (p. 216)

olfactory glomerulus (p. 216)

LEARNING OBJECTIVES FOR CHAPTER 8

When you have mastered the material in the chapter, you will
be able to:

LESSON 1: VISUAL AND AUDITORY SENSORY TRANSDUCTION

1. List all the sensory modalities of human beings and discuss the concept
    of sensory transduction.

2. Explain, in full detail, all the retinal processes (anatomical and
    physiological) involved in sensory transduction of visual stimuli.

3. Describe the anatomy of the ear and the cellular processes within the
    inner ear responsible for audition.

LESSON 2: SENSORY TRANSDUCTION IN THE OTHER SENSE MODALITIES

4. Describe the anatomy and physiology of the vestibular system.

5. Describe the anatomy and physiology of the receptor organs of the cutaneous senses and explain the peripheral mechanisms responsible for our sense of touch, temperature and pain.

6. Explain the peripheral mechanisms responsible for kinesthesia and organic sensitivity.

7. Describe the stimuli, receptors and mechanisms involved in taste (or gustation).

8. Describe the stimuli, receptors and peripheral mechanisms involved in olfaction.

LESSON 1: VISUAL AND AUDITORY SENSORY TRANSDUCTION

OBJECTIVE 8-1: List all the sensory modalities of human beings and discuss the concept of sensory transduction.

---

1. Why is sensory transduction necessary in order for organisms to interact with their environment? (p. 174)

2. Describe the two basic types of receptor cells involved in sensory transduction. Next to each, name the kind of electrical potential produced by each. (p. 175)

3. List the sensory modalities and explain why the vestibular sense is commonly not included in the list of the human senses. (p. 175)

OBJECTIVE 8-2: Explain in full detail all the retinal processes (anatomical and physiological) involved in sensory transduction of visual stimuli.

4. What is the electromagnetic spectrum? (pp. 176,177)

5. To which part of the spectrum are our eyes sensitive? (p. 177)

6. Explain how the iris changes the size of the pupil. (p. 177)

7. Explain why atropine (or belladonna) dilates the pupil. (p. 177)

8. Explain how the eye is able to focus both near and far objects on the retina. (p. 177)

9. Name the kinds of photoreceptors. Indicate the function of each and their location in the retina. (p. 177)

10. How do rods and cones differ in the way that they replace lamellae in their outer segments? (p. 179)

11. In the diagram of the human eye below, label the following: orbital bone, cornea, lens, ciliary muscle, pupil, iris, conjunctiva, retina, fovea, sclera, optic disk, inferior rectus muscle and superior rectus muscle. (p. 178)

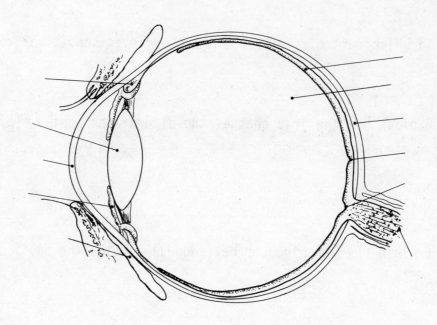

12. Give evidence that photoreceptors (particularly rods) are as sensitive to light as is physically possible. (p. 181)

13. Draw a rod and a cone showing the lamellae. (pp. 179,181)

14. List (or diagram), in order, the molecular events involved in visual transduction. Start from the point at which a photon strikes a molecule of rhodopsin and end your description with the hyperpolarization of the rod. Be precise and don't leave out any steps. (pp. 181,182)

15. Explain the role of cyclic nucleotides in receptor potentials of photoreceptors. (pp. 182,183)

16. Why are there four photopigments in the primate retina? (p. 184)

17. How many photopigments does one cone contain? (p. 184) _____

18. The axons of which retinal cells make up the optic nerve? (p. 185)

_____

19. Below is a diagram of retinal circuitry. Label the following cells: rods, cones, horizontal cells, bipolar cells, amacrine cells and ganglion cells. (p. 184)

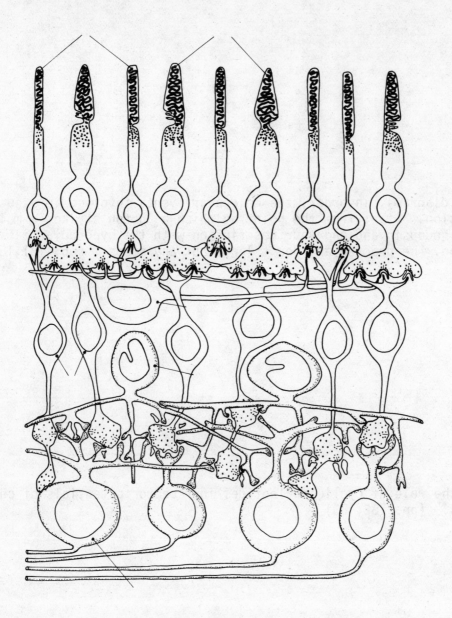

20. Using the above diagram, write, in your own words, the sequence of events involved in the transduction of visual stimuli. (pp. 180-185)

21. What two factors determine the size of the pupillary aperture? (p. 185)

_____

_____

22. Not only does the retina send neural messages to the brain, but the brain also sends information to the retina. Describe the aspects of vision that are controlled by efferent fibers. (pp. 185,186)

23. Describe what happened when Merton, in 1956, injected his eye with curare. What is the significance of this experiment? (p. 187)

24. Below, on the left, is a list of important terms you should know as a function of studying the section in the text on vision. Match the terms on the left to their best descriptions on the right. (pp. 176-187)

___ 1. 700 nanometers

___ 2. sclera

___ 3. conjunctiva

___ 4. cornea

___ 5. ciliary muscle

___ 6. retina

___ 7. rod

___ 8. cone

___ 9. fovea

___ 10. optic disk

___ 11. blind spot

___ 12. rhodopsin

___ 13. all-trans-retinal

___ 14. 11-cis-retinal

___ 15. ganglion cell

a. transparent outer layer of the front of the eye

b. photoreceptor, found most densely in the peripheral retina

c. central region of the retina

d. results from absence of photoreceptors at optic disk

e. where ganglion cell axons gather together to form the optic nerve

f. red

g. muscle that controls the shape of the lens

h. synthesized from vitamin A

i. retinal isomer formed by exposure to a photon

j. opaque outer coat of the eye

k. the axon of these retinal cells forms the optic nerve

l. unstable retinal isomer before interaction with a photon

m. photoreceptor which mediates color vision

n. photoreceptor surface on the back of the eye

o. mucous membrane lining of the eyelid

115

OBJECTIVE 8-3:   Describe the anatomy of the ear and the cellular
                 processes within the inner ear responsible for
                 audition.

25.   How are sound waves produced?   (pp. 187,188)

26.   Label the important auditory structures in the diagram below. (p. 188)

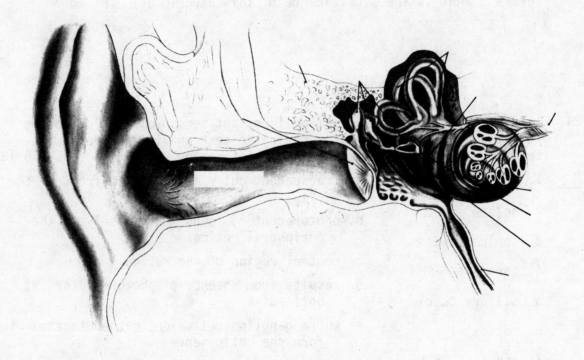

27.   Explain why the round window is necessary for the transmission of sound
      waves through the cochlea. (p. 189)

28. List, in order, the series of events that occurs from the time the tympanic membrane is set into vibration to the point where hair cells produce receptor potentials. (pp. 188,189)

29. Below is a diagram of the middle and inner ear. Label all the important structures, then trace the route of sound vibrations through the middle ear and cochlea. (pp. 189-191)

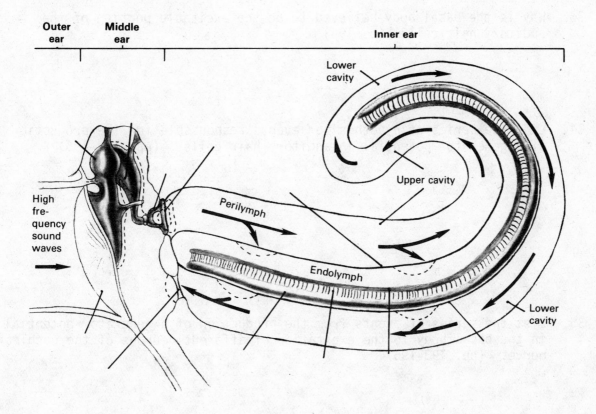

Outer ear   Middle ear   Inner ear

Lower cavity

High frequency sound waves

Perilymph

Upper cavity

Endolymph

Lower cavity

30. In the diagram on the preceding page, indicate where on the basilar membrane high and low frequencies cause maximum deformation. (p. 193)

31. Sensory transduction in the auditory system occurs when the basilar membrane is bent. Describe how physical energy vibrating the basilar membrane leads to neural activity. (p. 193)

32. What is the cochlear microphonic thought to represent? (p. 193)

33. Why is the basal body believed to be the excitable portion of the auditory hair cell? (p. 194)

34. List the series of hypothesized events responsible for the production of a generator potential in auditory hair cells. (pp. 193-195)

35. List the series of events from the production of a generator potential in the basal body to the excitation of afferent neurons of the cochlear nerve. (pp. 193-195)

36. What part of the afferent neuron receives transmitter substance from auditory hair cells? (p. 195) _____

Where are the cell bodies of the afferent fibers of the cochlear nerve located? (p. 195) _____

37. Although only 22% of the number of auditory hair cells are inner hair cells, why do we say that inner hair cells have primary importance in the transmission of auditory information to the CNS? (pp. 196,197)

38. What are the two means present in the human auditory system to control the nature of the sound waves that reach the oval window? (pp. 189,197)

39. While the role of efferent fiber to the auditory hair cells is unclear, do we know where the cell bodies of these fibers are located? (p. 197)

_____

40. Quiz yourself on the material on the auditory system. Below, on the left, is a list of important terms you should know as a function of studying the section in the text on audition. Match the term on the left to its best description on the right. (pp. 187-197)

____ 1. pinna
____ 2. tympanic membrane
____ 3. ossicle
____ 4. stapes
____ 5. cochlea
____ 6. tectorial membrane
____ 7. round window
____ 8. cochlear nerve
____ 9. endolymph
____ 10. cortilymph
____ 11. basal body
____ 12. spiral ganglion
____ 13. tensor tympani
____ 14. superior oli- vary nucleus

a. eardrum

b. contains the basilar membrane and hair cells

c. allows cochlear fluid to move back and forth

d. excitable portion of auditory receptor cells

e. liquid surrounding hair cells

f. outermost part of external ear

g. contains bipolar neuron of the cochlear nerve

h. contains cell bodies of auditory efferent fibers

i. middle ear bone which vibrates against oval window

j. a branch of the 8th cranial nerve

k. muscle of middle ear

l. liquid contained in scala media

m. rigid structure immediately above the basilar membrane

n. bone of the middle ear

119

LESSON 2: SENSORY TRANSDUCTION IN THE OTHER SENSE MODALITIES

OBJECTIVE 8-4: Describe the anatomy and physiology of the vestibular system.

Both the anatomy and the mechanics of the vestibular system are difficult to visualize and conceptualize. I would suggest that you read very carefully Pages 197-200, being sure to study each figure thoroughly. Then return here for some study questions.

41. Below is a diagram of the bony labyrinth of the inner ear. Label the cochlea, saccule, utricle, superior semicircular canal, posterior semicircular canal and lateral semicircular canal. Next to each label, indicate the information each structure gives us about our orientation in space. (pp. 197-200)

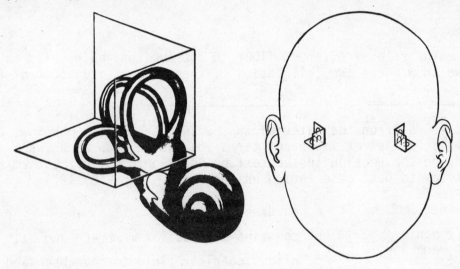

42. Now, using the above diagram, write, in your own words, a description of how the semicircular canals work. Make sure you include the words "ampulla, crista and endolymph" in your description. (pp. 198,199)

43. Explain what Steinhausen (1931) observed of the effects of angular acceleration on the semicircular canals. (p. 199)

44. There are two vestibular sacs, the _____ and the _____. Explain the structural relationship between the cilia and the otoconia within these two sacs. (pp. 199,200)

45. Explain how head movement activates the receptors within the utricle and saccule. (p. 201)

46. Below is a diagram showing Type I and Type II vestibular hair cells. Label each type and the important anatomical features of each. (pp. 200,201)

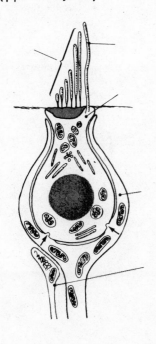 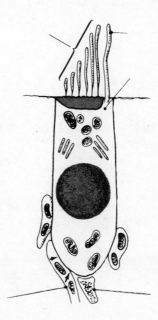

47. Below is a diagram showing how excitation and inhibition are produced by shearing force on vestibular hair cells. Explain, in your own words, the mechanisms involved. (p. 201)

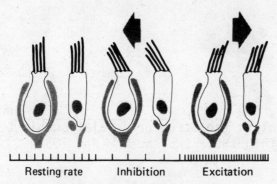

Resting rate   Inhibition   Excitation
Action potentials of vestibular axons

48. The hair cells of the semicircular canals are all oriented in one direction. Explain, using this fact, how information from the semi-circular canals of both ears together provides information about the magnitude and direction of angular rotation of the head. (p. 201)

49. Describe, using the following terms, the origin of the vestibular nerve: vestibular ganglion, fastigial nucleus, cerebellum, vestibular nuclei and medulla. (p. 202)

50. How does activity of vestibular efferent fibers affect the firing rate of afferent neurons? (p. 202)

OBJECTIVE 8-5: Describe the anatomy and physiology of the receptor organs of the cutaneous senses and explain the peripheral mechanisms responsible for our sense of touch, temperature and pain.

51. Name the two categories of the somatosenses. (p. 202)

a. _____   b. _____

52. Name the three categories of the cutaneous senses. (p. 203)

a. _____   _____

b. _____   _____

c. _____   _____

Next to each, name the type of receptor cell involved in each kind of sensitivity. (p. 203)

53. Name the four kinds of sensory endings in glabrous skin. (pp. 204,205)

a. _____   c. _____

b. _____   d. _____

54. Describe some of the problems we have in assigning a particular function to each kind of receptor. (p. 206)

55. Where are cold receptors located in the skin? Describe their structure. (p. 206)

56. Explain how Pacinian corpuscles are designed and how they detect pressure on the skin. (p. 207)

57. Draw and label a diagram of a Pacinian corpuscle and explain how a generator potential is produced. (pp. 205,207)

58. Draw and label the two types of mechanoreceptors associated with hairs within the skin. (pp. 204,207)

59. Using the diagram above, explain how Stetson's (1923) experiment showed that the free nerve ending near the surface of the skin is more sensitive. (p. 207)

60. Describe the structure of pain receptors (nocioceptors). (p. 208)

61. List the chemicals whose concentration within skin tissue has been correlated with pain. (p. 208)

62. By what two paths do somatosensory fibers enter the CNS? (p. 208)

a. _____   b. _____

```
┌─────────────────────────────────────────────────────────────┐
│  OBJECTIVE 8-6:  Explain the peripheral mechanisms responsible for │
│                  kinesthesia and organic sensitivity.         │
└─────────────────────────────────────────────────────────────┘
```

63. Define these terms. (pp. 208,209)

a. kinesthesia _____

b. organic sensitivity _____

64. Below is a diagram of a skeletal muscle. Label the structures important in our kinesthetic sense. (p. 210)

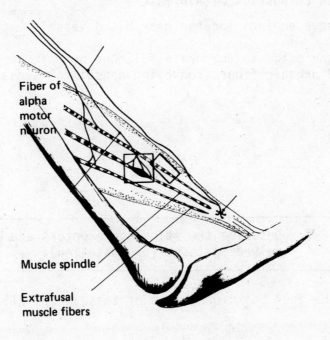

Fiber of
alpha
motor
neuron

Muscle spindle

Extrafusal
muscle fibers

65. The diagram below depicts the sensory endings associated with indivi-
    dual muscle fibers. Label the diagram and explain how sensory endings
    on intrafusal muscle fibers signal muscle length. (p. 210)

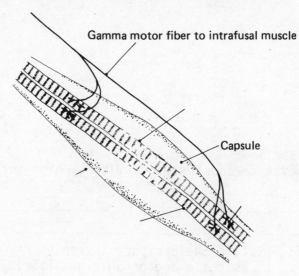

Gamma motor fiber to intrafusal muscle

Capsule

66. We are made aware of the position of our limbs and the state of our
    muscle by four kinds of information sent to the brain by muscle and
    tendon afferents. Next to each of the following receptors, indicate
    the kind of information they detect. (p. 209)

    a. Golgi tendon organ _____

    b. sensory endings on intrafusal muscle fibers _____

    c. Pacinian corpuscles within fascia _____

    d. free nerve endings located near blood vessels _____

67. Contrast the paths to the brain followed by pain sensitive organic
    fibers and organic fibers conveying nonpainful sensation. (pp. 210,211)

OBJECTIVE 8-7: Describe the stimuli, receptors and mechanisms in-
                volved in taste (or gustation).

---

68. What are the four basic qualities of taste? (p. 211)

    a. _____   c. _____

    b. _____   d. _____

126

69. How is the rich experience of flavor produced? (p. 211)

70. Describe, or draw, the structural relationship between taste buds and papillae. (pp. 211,212)

71. How is transduction of taste similar to the process of chemical transmission at synapses? (p. 213)

72. What are the common molecular characteristics of the following taste categories? (p. 213)

    a. sour _____

    b. salty _____

    c. bitter _____

    d. sweet _____

73. By what route do taste receptors of the front and back of the tongue, the pharynx and the larynx travel to the brain? (p. 213)

    a. anterior two-thirds of tongue _____

    b. posterior one-third of tongue _____

    c. pharynx _____

    d. larynx _____

```
OBJECTIVE 8-8:  Describe the stimuli, receptors and peripheral
                mechanisms involved in olfaction.
```

74. Where do the olfactory receptors reside? (p. 215) _____

    _____

75. Describe, or draw, the anatomy of the olfactory apparatus. Include the terms olfactory epithelium, turbinate bones, olfactory bulb and cribiform plate. (p. 215)

76. Draw a schematic diagram of olfactory receptors. Label the important structures and give a plausible explanation for how odor molecules produce generator potentials in these receptors. (pp. 215,216)

77. Explain the route of electrical information from the olfactory receptors to the olfactory bulb and olfactory nerve. (p. 216)

Thought Questions

1. While the visual and auditory systems seem very different, at a deeper conceptual level, they are really quite similar. This is especially true when considering the vibratory, or wavelike, properties of both visual and auditory stimuli. In what ways are these two sensory systems similar?

2. What might be the function of the inhibitory effect that CNS efferent fibers exert on vestibular neurons? In other words, under what kinds of conditions might it be useful to inhibit information entering the brain from the vestibular apparatus?

3. We humans appear to be consciously aware of sights, sounds, smells, tastes and pressure to the skin. Why do you suppose we are unaware of the very important functioning of the vestibular system? Try to frame your answer within the principle of natural selection and the psychological origins of conscious experience.

9

Sensory Coding

Essential Concepts

1. The nervous system has available only two basic formats by which to encode sensory stimulation -- spatial and temporal codes. Most sensory systems appear to use both codes.

2. The spatial relations of the retinal mosaic are maintained in both lateral geniculate nucleus and primary visual cortex. The second visual system, involving the superior colliculus and the secondary visual cortex, also uses a spatial code. The intensity of visual stimulation is coded by both the rate of firing of optic nerve fibers and spatially, by the two populations of photoreceptors, rods and cones. Color appears to be encoded by the presence of three different kinds of cones. The pattern of visual stimulation is encoded by feature detecting receptive fields of ganglion cells. The mechanism of lateral inhibition enhances contrast sensitivity and is important in feature specificity. Visual cortical cells also possess very specific response properties. Many cortical cells respond best to elongated moving bars or slits of light.

3. Two models of visual system coding currently prevail. Those favoring the edge-detector model argue that visual coding is done in a hierarchical, serial fashion with retinal ganglion receptive fields converging on simple cells in visual cortex and simple cells converging on complex cells to produce more complex receptive fields. However, there is much evidence that visual receptive fields respond to spatial frequencies. Some visual physiologists argue that the visual system is a parallel processing Fourier analyzer of the visual world.

4. The basilar membrane is spatially represented in a tonotopic fashion on auditory cortex. In this way, the sensory code for pitch is also spatially coded. There is evidence that lateral inhibition between hair cells in the basilar membrane enhances the sharpness of frequency tuning. Very low frequencies of sound stimulation appear to be temporally encoded. The intensity of auditory stimuli is spatially encoded in

auditory cortex by vertical distance from the cortical surface.

5. The lemniscal system conveys precisely localized information from touch receptors. The spinothalamic system carries pain and temperature sensation. The somatotopic organization of the skin in both the thalamus and primary somatosensory cortex codes the location of the stimulation. From the thalamus, most pain and temperature fibers project to secondary somatosensory cortex. Frequency of stimulation is encoded by two types of receptors. Low frequency detection is performed by quickly adapting mechanoreceptors in the surface of the skin. Higher frequencies are detected by Pacinian corpuscles in deep tissue. Coolness and warmth are detected by different receptors and the responses of both combine at higher neural levels to provide thermal sensation.

6. Taste fibers synapse in the solitary nucleus of the medulla. Second-order neurons synapse on neurons in the thalamus, which, in turn, project to several areas of cortex. A given taste fiber is sensitive to more than one taste quality, suggesting that the psychological dimension of taste depends upon central analysis of patterns of activity in many neurons.

7. The axons of olfactory nerves project to limbic cortex without synapsing in thalamus. A plausible theory of olfaction is that primary odors can be characterized by seven different molecular configurations recognized by receptive sites of similar shape in olfactory hair cells.

Key Words

sensory coding (p. 219)

spatial coding (p. 220)

line-specific coding (p. 220)

temporal coding (p. 220)

epiphenomenon (p. 221)

homunculus (p. 222)

optic radiations (p. 224)

calcarine fissure (p. 224)

striate cortex (p. 224)

retinotopic organization (p. 224)

visual prosthesis (p. 224)

scotoma (p. 224)

optic chiasm (p. 224)

decussation (p. 224)

dorsal lateral geniculate nucleus (p. 224)

suprachiasmatic nucleus (p. 227)

accessory optic nucleus (p. 227)

pretectum (p. 227)

superior colliculus (p. 227)

ventral lateral geniculate nucleus (p. 227)

nonlinear (p. 228)

Limulus (p. 228)

receptive field (p. 229)

receptive field mapping (p. 229)

X cell (p. 230)

Y cell (p. 230)

simple cell (p. 231)

complex cell (p. 231)

2-deoxyglucose (p. 233)

ocular dominance (p. 234)

retinal disparity (p. 237)

fixation plane (p. 237)

feature detection (p. 237)

sine-wave grating (p. 239)

spatial frequency (p. 239)

visual angle (p. 239)

Fourier analysis (p. 239)

serial processing (p. 242)

parallel processing (p. 242)

nucleus of the solitary tract (p. 274)

parabrachial nucleus (p. 274)

thalamic taste area (p. 274)

anterior insular cortex (p. 275)

lateral olfactory tract (p. 276)

limbic cortex (p. 276)

stereospecific theory (p. 277)

LEARNING OBJECTIVES FOR CHAPTER 9

When you have mastered the material in the chapter, you will be able to:

LESSON 1: SENSORY CODING AND THE VISUAL SYSTEM

1. Explain, and give examples of, spatial and temporal coding.

2. Explain how retinotopic organization is maintained throughout the ascending visual system from retina to visual cortex.

3. Describe the receptive field organization of each level of the retino-geniculo-striate visual pathway.

4. Explain how ocular dominance columns are formed and describe their functional significance.

5. Describe the controversy between and the evidence for the "edge detector" and "spatial frequency" theories of visual perception.

6. Describe the role of visual plasticity and inferotemporal cortex in complex pattern recognition, visual learning and visual memory.

7. Explain what we know about how the visual system codes color.

LESSON 2: CODING IN THE AUDITORY SYSTEM

8. Diagram the auditory pathway from the cochlea to the auditory cortex.

9. Explain how the auditory system uses both spatial and temporal coding to code for auditory frequency (or pitch).

10. Explain how the auditory system codes the intensity or loudness of auditory stimuli.

11. Explain how the auditory system is able to encode the location of auditory stimuli.

LESSON 3: CODING OF THE OTHER SENSE MODALITIES

12. Describe the anatomical pathways of the vestibular system and the reflexes that these pathways mediate.

13. Diagram the anatomical pathways of the lemniscal and spinothalamic systems.

14. Describe the neural codes used by the somatosensory system.

15. Describe the neural pathway and neural codes used in gustation.

16. Describe the neural pathway and neural codes used in olfaction.

LESSON 1: SENSORY CODING AND THE VISUAL SYSTEM

> OBJECTIVE 9-1: Explain, and give examples of, spatial and temporal coding.

1. Why does the nervous system need sensory codes? (pp. 219,220)

2. Only relatively simple codes can be transmitted by single neurons. How is the intensity of a stimulus encoded by a single neuron? (p. 220)

3. What are the two basic formats of coding available to the nervous system? Give an example of each. (p. 220)

4. Describe another temporal code besides rate or frequency. (pp. 220,221)

5. How can we know that a candidate neural code is actually the one used by the nervous system and not simply an epiphenomenon? (p. 221)

6. Explain why the search for the "homunculus" in the brain is not a productive means for understanding our sensory experience. (p. 222)

OBJECTIVE 9-2: Explain how retinotopic organization is maintained throughout the ascending visual system from retina to visual cortex.

---

7. Why is the retina said to have a mosaic organization? (p. 222)

8. Contrast the photoreceptor-to-ganglion cell axon relations in the fovea and the peripheral retina. (p. 223)

9. How do these relations correlate with the acuity of vision in the peripheral versus foveal retina? (p. 223)

10. Trace the visual pathway from optic nerve to visual cortex. (pp. 223, 224)

11. Explain how the retinotopic organization of the visual pathway serves as a sensory code. (p. 224)

12. Give two pieces of evidence that support the idea that retinotopic organization is truly a spatial code used by the visual system. (p. 224)

13. The retinal mosaic is not equally represented in cortex. Which part of the retina is most represented? (p. 224) _____

14. On the following page is a diagram of the primary visual pathways. Label the diagram, then show how partial decussation at the optic chiasm insures that each lateral geniculate nucleus and each visual cortex receives ganglion cell axons from half of each visual field. (pp. 224,225)

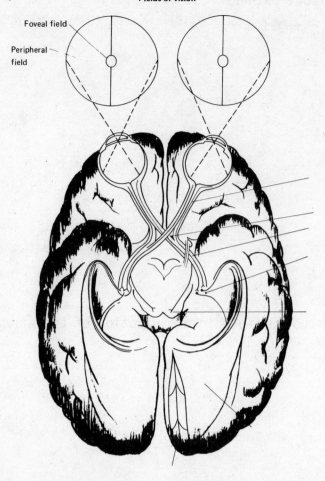

Fields of vision

Foveal field

Peripheral field

15. Besides the primary retino-geniculo-striate pathway, the retina sends information to five other areas of the brain. Name these areas and indicate the function of each visual pathway. (p. 227)

16. Explain why the range of brightness to which the visual system is sensitive cannot be coded by neural firing rate. (p. 227)

17. Explain two ways in which the eye codes the large range of stimulus intensities. (pp. 227,228)

18. Give evidence that, beyond the level of the photoreceptors, the visual system does not respond to absolute brightness. (pp. 228,229)

OBJECTIVE 9-3: Describe the receptive field organization of each level of the retino-geniculo-striate visual pathway.

---

19. What is the receptive field of a neuron and how is it mapped in the visual system? (p. 229)

20. What did Kuffler (1953) discover about the receptive field organization of the cat retina? (p. 229)

21. What is the resulting response when both center and surround of a receptive field are simultaneously stimulated by light? (p. 229)

22. Differentiate the physiology and anatomy of X and Y cells. (p. 230)

23. Describe the receptive fields of neurons in the following levels of the visual system. (pp. 229-231)

    a. retina

    b. LGN

    c. Layer IV of striate cortex

24. Explain, in a diagram, Hubel and Wiesel's model of the neural circuitry that produces the receptive field of a "simple cell". (p. 231)

25. Describe the receptive field of a "complex cell". (pp. 231,232)

26. Explain, in a diagram, Hubel and Wiesel's model of the neural circuitry that produces the receptive field of a "complex cell". (pp. 231,232)

27. Explain the rationale, procedure and results of Hubel, Wiesel and Stryker's (1978) 2-deoxyglucose experiment. (pp. 233,234)

28. Now, describe how receptive fields are distributed in the various layers of visual cortex. (pp. 232-234)

29. What do we mean when we say that visual neurons have an "eye preference"? (p. 234)

30. Describe the autoradiographic procedure used to demonstrate the existence of ocular dominance columns. (pp. 236,237)

31. Explain how binocular visual cells and retinal disparity are important in depth perception. (p. 237)

32. What evidence suggests that there are two classes of cells that respond to retinal disparity? (p. 237)

OBJECTIVE 9-5: Describe the controversy between and the evidence for the "edge detector" and "spatial frequency" theories of visual perception.

33. Describe Hubel and Wiesel's edge detector model of the visual system. (pp. 237-239)

34. What are the two assumptions of this model? (pp. 237-239)

35. Explain what we mean by "spatial frequency". (p. 239)

36. What is a Fourier analysis of a slice of a visual scene? (pp. 239,240)

37. Explain why the fact that neurons in the visual cortex respond best to a particular spatial frequency is evidence that the visual system performs a Fourier analysis of the visual world. (pp. 240,241)

38. Explain how Blakemore and Campbell (1969) used the technique of adaptation to test the spatial frequency theory of the visual system. (p. 241)

39. How did Harmon and Julesz (1973) demonstrate the importance of low spatial frequencies in recognizing visual patterns? (p. 241)

40. Look at the two pictures of Lincoln on page 242. Which of the photographs has had high-frequency information added to it? What point were Harmon and Julesz (1973) trying to make about the human visual system in this demonstration? (pp. 241, 242)

41. Contrast the edge detector and spatial frequency models of the visual system. (pp. 237-242)

42. How can the two theories be reconciled with one another? (p. 242)

43. Why is Hubel and Wiesel's model considered to be a serial one? (p. 242)

44. What evidence suggests that serial processing is not the mechanism used in higher level visual coding? (pp. 242,243)

45. How are X and Y cells and simple and complex cells related? (p. 243)

```
OBJECTIVE 9-6:  Describe the role of visual plasticity and infero-
                temporal cortex in complex pattern recognition,
                visual learning and visual memory.
```

46. Describe the experiment by Hirsch and Spinelli (1971) that demonstrated that visual experience could modify the receptive fields of neurons in the visual cortex of the kitten. (pp. 243-245)

47. What is the effect of discordant binocular visual experience on binocular receptive fields in visual cortex? (p. 245)

48. What is "psychic blindness"? How is it experimentally produced?
(p. 245)

49. Give electrophysiological support for the hypothesis that inferotemporal cortex has an important role in complex analysis of visual information in the primate. (p. 246)

50. Give evidence that the superior colliculus also is involved in visual pattern recognition. (p. 246)

OBJECTIVE 9-7: Explain what we know about how the visual system codes color.

---

51. Describe the three-cone theory and the opponent color theory of color vision. (p. 247)

52. What physiological evidence supports the three-cone theory? (p. 247)

53. The opponent color theory better describes the activity of retinal ganglion cells. What aspects of the receptive field organization of these cells support this theory of color vision? (pp. 247,248)

54. a. Describe the receptive field organization of neurons in the lateral geniculate. (pp. 248,249)

    b. Which theory of color coding does this receptive field organization support? (pp. 248,249) _____

55. Describe what we know about color coding in visual cortex. What are the problems in attempting to study cortical color coding? (pp. 249-251)

LESSON 2: CODING IN THE AUDITORY SYSTEM

OBJECTIVE 9-8: Diagram the auditory pathway from the cochlea to auditory cortex.

56. Look at Figure 9.22 in the text. In the space provided on the following page, draw a simplified wiring diagram of the auditory system. Include the cochlea, cochlear nuclei, superior olivary nuclei, lateral lemniscus, inferior colliculi, medial geniculate nuclei and auditory cortices. (pp. 251,252)

```
┌─────────────────────────────────────────────────────────────────┐
│  OBJECTIVE 9-9:  Explain how the auditory system uses both spatial │
│                  and temporal coding to code for auditory frequency │
│                  (or pitch).                                        │
└─────────────────────────────────────────────────────────────────┘
```

57. Name the kind of organization in the auditory system that is analogous
    to retinotopic organization. (p. 252)

    _____

58. What happens psychologically when the frequency of a sound stimulus is
    increased? (p. 252)

59. As you learned in the last section, the visual system uses a spatial
    code. Explain how the organization of the basilar membrane codes
    auditory stimuli spatially. (pp. 252,253)

60. Draw a frequency tuning curve of an auditory nerve fiber. Label the axes. (p. 253)

61. Explain how lateral inhibition may be the mechanism responsible for sharpening the frequency tuning characteristics of auditory hair cells and nerve fibers. (pp. 253-255)

62. Show diagrammatically how lateral inhibition works. (p. 254)

63. How did Kiang (1965) demonstrate that spatial encoding mechanisms cannot explain how the auditory system encodes very low frequencies? (p. 256)

64. Explain why Miller and Taylor's (1948) experiment demonstrates that the auditory system can also use a temporal code for pitch. (p. 256)

65. Below is a frequency histogram of an auditory nerve fiber stimulated with a 412-Hz tone. Explain how this plot was constructed and what it means. (pp. 256,257)

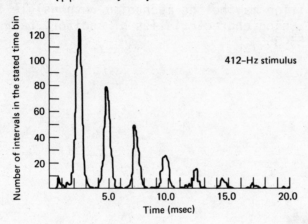

66. Explain how frequency histograms of the firing of auditory nerve fibers give credence to the volley theory of temporal coding of pitch. (pp. 256-258)

67. Rods have been shown, under special conditions, to be responsive to one
    photon. Describe the analogous sensitivity in the auditory system.
    (p. 258)

68. Not only frequency, but also intensity of auditory stimuli is encoded
    spatially in auditory cortex. Describe how intensity is spatially
    represented. (pp. 259,260)

69. What tentative conclusions can we make from lesion experiments con-
    cerning the function of auditory cortex in the analysis of sound?
    (p. 260)

70. Explain how phase differences in each ear can supply information about
    the location of the stimulus source. (p. 261)

71. Describe or diagram Licklider's (1959) neural model that accounts for auditory localization. (p. 262)

72. What are the two mechanisms used by the auditory system to localize sounds? (pp. 260-262)

73. Explain how the auditory system localizes high frequency sounds. (p. 262)

74. Why is it that we normally do not hear the echoes of everyday noises? (pp. 262-263)

OBJECTIVE 9-12: Describe the anatomical pathways of the vestibular
system and the reflexes that these pathways mediate.

75. List the areas of the brain to which information from the vestibular
sacs and semicircular canals travels. Next to each structure, indicate
the function and effects of vestibular stimulation. (pp. 263-265)

OBJECTIVE 9-13: Diagram the anatomical pathways of the lemniscal
and spinothalamic systems.

76. Name the two pathways involved in the cutaneous senses and indicate
what information is carried by each. (p. 265)

77. On the following page is a diagram of lemniscal pathways. Label the
major nuclei and axonal pathways. (p. 266)

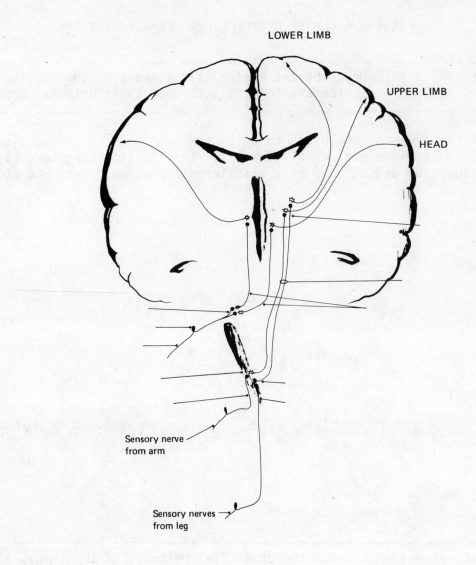

LOWER LIMB

UPPER LIMB

HEAD

Sensory nerve
from arm

Sensory nerves
from leg

78. What aspect of the lemniscal system is responsible for the fact that cutaneous stimulation from one side of the body travels to the opposite side of the brain? (p. 265)

79. On the following page is a diagram of the spinothalamic pathway. Label the major nuclei and axonal pathways. Trace the flow of information from skin through each level of the spinal cord and the brain. (pp. 266,267)

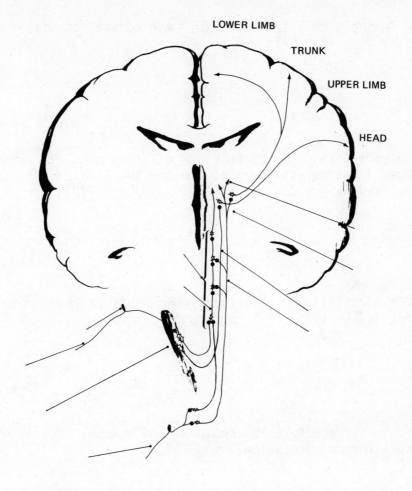

LOWER LIMB

TRUNK

UPPER LIMB

HEAD

OBJECTIVE 9-14: Describe the neural codes used by the somatosensory
system.

---

80. Why is the somatotopic organization of somatosensory cortex an example
of spatial coding? (p. 268)

81. Describe the receptive field organization of neurons in somatosensory
cortex. (pp. 268,269)

82. What is the mechanism responsible for adaptation within the cutaneous senses? (pp. 270,271)

83. Touch receptors, like other kinds of receptors, are most sensitive to changes in stimulation. What are the two classes of touch receptors postulated by Mountcastle (1967)? (pp. 272,273)

84. How do cortical and subcortical components of the somatosensory system differ in how they code frequency of cutaneous stimulation? (p. 273)

85. How do skin receptors for coolness and warmth combine their inputs to produce thermal sensation? (p. 273)

OBJECTIVE 9-15: Describe the neural pathway and neural codes used in gustation.

---

86. Describe the anatomical pathway from the tongue to all levels of the brain. (pp. 274,275)

87. How is the sensation of taste coded? (pp. 275,276)

┌───┐
│   OBJECTIVE 9-16: Describe the neural pathways and neural codes used │
│   in olfaction.   │
└───┘

88. Which areas of the brain receive olfactory information? (pp. 276,277)

89. In what way is the neural pathway of olfactory input to cortex differ-
     ent from the other senses? (pp. 276,277)

90. Describe and evaluate Amoore's theory of olfaction. (pp. 277,278)

Thought Questions

1. Suppose you were Hubel and Wiesel. How would you explain our ability to
    visually analyze the photograph on Page 240? From what you've learned
    about the "edge detector" and "spatial frequency" theories, which do you
    think is more reasonable?

2. Do you think the specific and complex receptive fields of visual neurons
    in inferotemporal cortex result from learning (visual plasticity as in
    visual cortex), or are animals born with these complex receptive fields?

3. If you had to choose being either blind or deaf, which would you choose?

157

10

Glands, Muscles, and the Control of Movement

Essential Concepts

1. The brain interacts with the environment through the effectors of the body, glands and muscles.

2. Exocrine glands, such as the lachrymal gland, salivary gland, sweat gland and gall bladder, secrete their products through ducts to the outside of the body. Endocrine glands, such as the ovaries, testes and thyroid gland, secrete their products into the blood system to affect other organs of the body. Both types of glands are controlled by the brain, while the brain is affected by the secretions of a variety of glands.

3. The hypothalamus produces a number of releasing and inhibiting hormones that regulate the synthesis and release of anterior pituitary hormones that, in turn, stimulate the production and release of hormones in other endocrine glands. The hypothalamic-hypophyseal portal system carries hypothalamic substances to the anterior pituitary. Anterior pituitary hormones are proteins that stimulate their target cells by interacting with receptors on the surface of these cells.

4. The other effectors of the body, skeletal, smooth and cardiac muscles, are also controlled by the brain. Skeletal muscle contractions are directly stimulated by alpha motor neurons in the ventral horn of the spinal cord. End plate potentials in muscle fibers are caused by the interaction of acetylcholine released from the alpha motor neuron axon terminal with receptor proteins in the muscle fiber membrane. The uptake of calcium ions into the muscle fiber induces muscle proteins, actin and myosin, to alternately bind and unbind, causing contraction of the muscle fiber.

5. Muscle spindles or stretch receptors detect stretch in the muscle while the Golgi tendon organ detects tension in the tendon connecting the muscle to the bone. The monosynaptic reflex, important in the maintenance

of posture, involves the stimulation of stretch receptors that indirectly induces the muscle to contract.

6. The gamma motor system, by sending efferent axons to muscle spindles, determines the length of these sensory endings and, thus, indirectly, the length of the entire muscle. The gamma system controls muscle tone.

7. Motor cortex, the basal ganglia and the cerebellum control the contraction of muscles by stimulating alpha and gamma motor neurons. It used to be thought that the pyramidal system, beginning in motor cortex and ending in the spinal cord, was responsible for the initiation of voluntary movements. However, lesions of the pyramidal system do not result in paralysis but, rather, in a weakness in muscle strength. From clinical evidence in humans, association cortex appears to be important in the initiation of movement, while the pyramidal system seems to be more involved in the control of fine movements of the fingers and hands in response to tactile input.

8. The extrapyramidal system is crucial in the control of starting and stopping of movement. Humans with damage to the basal ganglia can usually walk, but have difficulty in starting and stopping the sequence. The corticorubrospinal system, considered as part of the extrapyramidal system, cooperates with the pyramidal system. Damage to both the pyramidal and corticorubrospinal pathways results in a complete loss of movement.

9. While the basal ganglia are involved in the generation of slow ramp movements, the cerebellum plays a very important role in programming rapid movements.

Key Words

effector (p. 281)

endocrine gland (p. 282)

exocrine gland (p. 282)

hypothalamic-hypophyseal portal system (p. 283)

anterior pituitary gland (p. 283)

trophic hormone (p. 284)

target cell (p. 284)

steroid hormone (p. 284)

posterior pituitary (p. 284)

skeletal muscle (p. 285)

flexion/extension (p. 285)

LEARNING OBJECTIVES FOR CHAPTER 10

When you have mastered the material in the chapter, you will be able to:

LESSON 1: GLANDS, MUSCLES AND SPINAL REFLEXES

1. Explain how the central nervous system controls the secretion of glands.

2. Describe the anatomy and function of the three types of muscle.

3. Describe the structure of skeletal muscle and the chemistry of muscle contraction.

4. Explain the monosynaptic and polysynaptic mechanisms responsible for reflexive control of movement.

5. Explain the function and mechanism of the gamma motor system.

6. Explain the concept of recurrent inhibition.

LESSON 2: THE PYRAMIDAL AND EXTRAPYRAMIDAL MOTOR SYSTEMS

7. Describe the anatomy and function of the pyramidal motor system in the control of skeletal muscle contraction and movement.

8. Describe the anatomy of the extrapyramidal system and explain its role in the control and initiation of movement.

9. Explain the cerebellum's role in motor control.

LESSON 1: GLANDS, MUSCLES AND SPINAL REFLEXES

OBJECTIVE 10-1: Explain how the central nervous system controls the secretion of glands.

---

1. Why are both muscle fibers and secretory cells considered to be effectors? (p. 281)

2. Name the two types of glands. (p. 282)

_____

_____

3. Endocrine and exocrine glands are different in a variety of ways. Indicate whether the terms or statements on the left are descriptive of endocrine or exocrine glands, or both. (pp. 282,283)

a. secretion controlled by sphincter _____

b. neurotransmitter-like secretion _____

c. secretion controlled by brain _____

d. gall bladder _____

e. "outside-secreting" _____

f. seminal gland _____

g. "inside-secreting" _____

h. sweat gland _____

i. lachrymal gland _____

j. controlled by hypothalamic hormones _____

k. secrete hormones into capillaries _____

4. Below is a diagram of the pituitary gland, showing the portal blood system. Label the important features, then trace how the hypothalamus controls the release of hormones from the anterior pituitary. (p. 283)

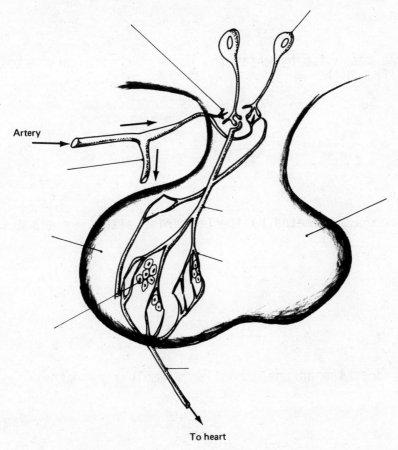

Artery

To heart

163

5. Why are most of the anterior pituitary hormones called trophic hormones? (p. 284)

6. What kind of molecules are anterior pituitary hormones? (p. 284)

   _____

7. How are these molecules able to produce their effects on their target cells elsewhere in the body? (p. 284)

8. How does the molecular structure of anterior pituitary hormones differ from steroid hormones? (p. 284)

9. Describe the mechanism by which the posterior pituitary releases its hormones. (p. 284)

10. Name two hormones secreted by the posterior pituitary and describe their functions. (p. 284)

11. In what way does the adrenal medulla resemble a sympathetic ganglion? (p. 284)

12. What substances does the adrenal medulla secrete? (p. 284)

13. What are the physiological results of adrenal stimulation? (p. 284)

OBJECTIVE 10-2: Describe the anatomy and the function of the three types of muscle.

---

14. How are skeletal muscles fastened to bone? (p. 285)

15. Give examples of the two major movements mediated by skeletal muscle. (p. 285)

16. What part of the nervous system controls smooth muscles? (p. 285)

_____

17. Give some examples of the role of multiunit smooth muscle. (p. 285)

18. How is the activity of single-unit smooth muscle different from that of multi-unit muscle? (p.285)

19. In what way does cardiac muscle display single-unit type of activity? (p. 285)

OBJECTIVE 10-3: Describe the structure of skeletal muscle and the chemistry of muscle contraction.

---

20. Below is a schematic diagram showing the anatomy of skeletal muscle. Label the following and, next to each label, indicate the function of each structure: extrafusal muscle fiber, intrafusal muscle fiber, alpha motor neuron, Golgi tendon organ and muscle spindle. (p. 286)

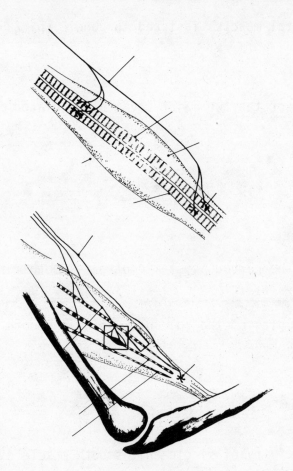

21. Roughly how many muscle fibers are controlled by an alpha motor neuron in the eye? _____ How many muscle fibers are innervated by one alpha motor neuron in the muscles of the leg? _____ What is a motor unit? (p. 287)

22. Order the following components of striated muscle from the smallest
    subcomponent to the largest. (pp. 286,287)

        myofibril

        actin/myosin

        motor unit

        muscle fiber

        extrafusal muscle fiber

23. The synapse between an efferent nerve terminal and the membrane of a
    muscle fiber is called a _____. (p. 287)

24. On what part of muscle fibers do nerve terminals synapse? (p. 287)

    _____

25. What transmitter substance is released at the neuromuscular junction?
    (p. 287) _____

26. How do end plate potentials (EPPs) in muscle fibers differ from EPSPs
    in the CNS? (p. 287)

27. Explain what we mean when we say that the final decision making occurs
    at the level of the motor neuron and not in the muscle. (p. 287)

28. What membrane permeability changes occur at the muscle fiber during an
    EPP? (pp. 287,288)

29. Describe what happens inside the muscle fiber to produce muscle fiber contraction. (pp. 288,289)

30. What determines the strength of a muscle contraction? (p. 289)

```
┌──────────────────────────────────────────────────────────────────────┐
│ OBJECTIVE 10-4:  Explain the monosynaptic and polysynaptic mechan-     │
│                  isms responsible for reflexive control of movement.   │
└──────────────────────────────────────────────────────────────────────┘
```

31. Intrafusal muscle fibers contain sensory endings that are sensitive to
_____.
These sensory endings are excited when the muscle is _____.
Golgi tendon organs are located in _____ and
detect the amount of _____ exerted by the muscle
on the tendon. (p. 289)

32. Draw a diagram showing the muscular and spinal components of the mono-synaptic stretch reflex. Label the important features in your diagram. (p. 292)

33. Using your diagram on the preceding page, explain, step by step, why a tap on the patella results in leg extension. (pp. 291,292)

34. Explain the utility of the monosynaptic stretch reflex in maintaining an upright posture. (pp. 292,293)

35. Explain in a drawing the concepts of neural divergence and convergence. (pp. 293,294)

36. Draw a diagram showing the anatomical features of the Golgi tendon reflex. Label the diagram, then explain how Golgi tendon organs are able to inhibit muscle contraction. (pp. 293,294)

37. What is the function of the GTO reflex? (p. 294)

38. Explain why the clasp-knife reflex occurs in decerebrate cats.
    (pp. 294,295)

39. Label the diagram below, showing the relation between agonist and
    antagonist muscles. Then, using the diagram, explain the neural mech-
    anism by which antagonistic muscles relax when the agonist muscle is
    excited. (p. 295)

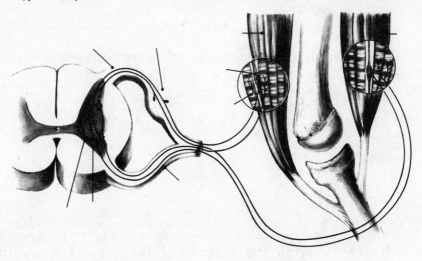

40. Why is the above mechanism necessary for limb movement? (p. 295)

OBJECTIVE 10-5: Explain the function and mechanism of the gamma motor system.

41. What is the function of the gamma motor system? (p. 296)

42. How does it work? (p. 296)

43. What is muscle tone? (p. 297)

44. Explain how the gamma motor system maintains muscle tone. (p. 297)

45. How is the function of the gamma motor system exemplified in the Jendrassic maneuver? (p. 297)

OBJECTIVE 10-6: Explain the concept of recurrent inhibition.

46. On the following page is a diagram showing recurrent inhibition in the spinal cord. Label the diagram. (p. 298)

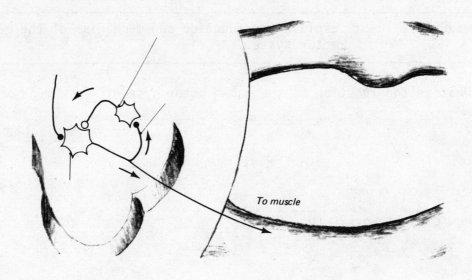

To muscle

47. Explain how recurrent collaterals are involved in self-initiated inhibition of alpha motor neurons. (p. 298)

48. What is the adaptive value of this kind of recurrent inhibition? (p. 298)

LESSON 2: THE PYRAMIDAL AND EXTRAPYRAMIDAL MOTOR SYSTEMS

OBJECTIVE 10-7: Describe the anatomy and function of the pyramidal motor system in the control of skeletal muscle contraction and movement.

49. Why is it, strictly speaking, incorrect to say that movements other than reflex movements are "voluntary"? (p. 300)

50. What is the motor homunculus? How is the organization of motor cortex similar to somatosensory cortex? (p. 301)

51. Below is a diagram of the pyramidal motor system pathway. Label the diagram and trace the flow of motor commands from cortex to alpha motor neuron. (pp. 302,303)

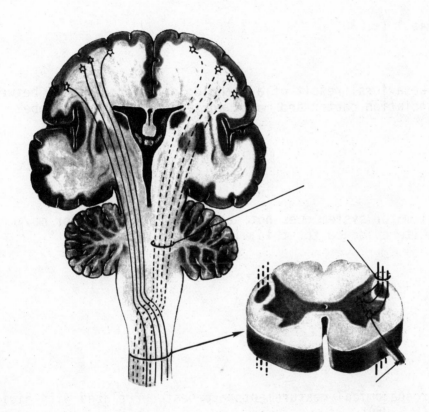

52. Explain why damage to the right motor cortex will result in motor impairments on the left side of the body. (p. 302)

53. How do we know that voluntary movements do not originate in the pre-central gyrus? (p. 303)

54. Where might voluntary movements originate? Cite evidence for your answer. (p. 303)

55. Define apraxia. (p. 303)

56. What is the behavioral result of a pathological disconnection between auditory association cortex and motor cortex of the frontal lobe? (pp. 303,304)

57. The pyramidal motor system does not seem to be essential for movement in humans. Cite evidence for this view. (p. 304)

58. What two neuroanatomical measurements are best correlated with digital dexterity? (p. 305)

_____

_____

Explain the significance of these correlations. (p. 305)

59. Describe Evarts' neurophysiological experiments in the motor cortex of monkeys. What is the significance of these results? (p. 305)

60. Towe and Zimmerman (1973) stimulated the motor cortex of monkeys, transected the pyramidal tracts, and then stimulated motor cortex again. What did they find? (p. 306)

61. What does Kornhuber believe to be the role of motor cortex and the pyramidal system? (p. 307)

Give four pieces of evidence that support his point of view. (p. 307)

OBJECTIVE 10-8: Describe the anatomy of the extrapyramidal system and explain its role in the control and initiation of movement.

---

62. Cite evidence from lesion and stimulation experiments that the globus pallidus has a facilitory role in motor control while the caudate nucleus has an inhibitory role. (p. 308)

63. Below is a schematic diagram showing the extrapyramidal pathways.
Label the diagram and trace the flow of motor information among cortex,
basal ganglia, thalamus, red nucleus and the spinal cord. (pp. 308,309)

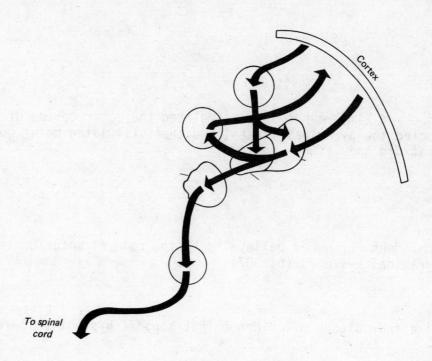

64. Make a general statement about the role of the basal ganglia in motor
programming and the initiation of movements. (p. 309)

65. Describe the symptoms of Parkinson's disease. (p. 309)

66. What is the anatomical problem in Parkinsonian patients? (p. 309)

67. Indicate on the diagram in Question #63 the pathways of the corticorubrospinal system. (pp. 309,310)

68. What is the result of damage to both the pyramidal tracts and the corticorubrospinal system? (p. 310)

69. Discuss the role of the reticulospinal fibers in tonic control of muscles. (p. 310)

70. Kornhuber has suggested that the basal ganglia are involved in the generation of slow ramp movements. What clinical evidence supports his view? (p. 310)

What neurophysiological evidence also supports this view? (p. 310)

OBJECTIVE 10-9: Explain the cerebellum's role in motor control.

71. What are the three major functions of the cerebellum in motor control? (p. 311)

a.

b.

c.

72. The cerebellum seems to be intimately involved in precisely programming rapid and complex movements that are too fast for feedback. Give two original examples of such complex movements. (p. 311)

73. Below is a schematic diagram of cerebellar inputs and outputs. Label the diagram and explain the function of each component. (p. 312)

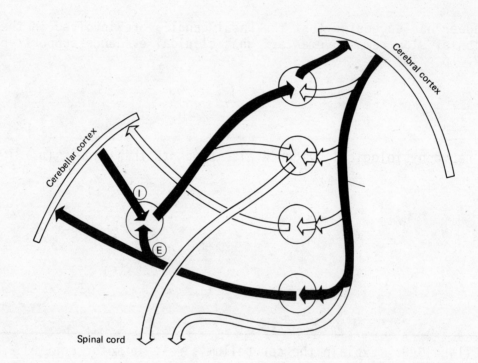

74. What is the result of unilateral neocerebellar lesions in humans? (p. 313)

75. What are saccadic eye movements? (p. 313)

What effect does cerebellar damage have on saccadic eye movements?
(p. 313)

76. What other evidence suggests that the cerebellar cortex controls rapid
skilled movements? (p. 313)

77. What evidence argues that the deep cerebellar nuclei are involved in
stopping and holding movements? (p. 313)

Thought Questions

1. Can you think of a better terminology to distinguish between reflexes
and "voluntary" movement? Do you think animals other than humans are
capable of "voluntary" movement?

2. If you had to choose between having brain damage in motor cortex, the
basal ganglia or the cerebellum, which would you choose? Why?

3. Have you ever been driving a car on a highway for many minutes before
you realize you have been completely unconscious of doing so? What
motor mechanisms do you think might be involved in this kind of complex but automatic movement?

11

Sexual Development and Behavior

Essential Concepts

1. Sex hormones have a dual role in the control of sexual behavior. They have an organizational effect that shapes the ultimate development of an organism's sexual organs and brain. Sex hormones also have an activational effect. They influence and maintain the functioning of adult sex organs as well as the expression of adult sexual behavior.

2. Regardless of chromosomal sex, mammals contain, during early fetal life, the primordial organs for both sexes. Early in development, a pair of primitive, potentially bisexual, gonads will develop into testes if a Y chromosome is present or into ovaries of two X chromosomes are present.

3. The presence of a Y chromosome prevents the development of a female body. Without prenatal secretion of androgens from the testes, the brain and body will be born female. Prenatal androgens predispose organisms to male behavior (regardless of genetic sex), whereas their absence predisposes the organism towards female behavior. Nature's "impulse" is to create a female.

4. Sex differences in brain function are seen in the hypothalamic control of pituitary release of gonadotrophic hormones. The output of gonadotrophins by the anterior pituitary is cyclic in females and relatively constant in males. The nonandrogenized cycling brain responds to estrogen by releasing luteinizing hormone releasing hormone which causes the LH surge that causes ovulation.

5. Early androgenization of females or early castration of males influences later sexual preferences. Early androgenization of female children appears to have both physiological and behavioral effects. However, a case of accidental penile ablation in one male infant illustrates that changes in gender identification can be made through unambiguous parental re-assignment of sex role in early childhood.

6. Humans, contrary to common belief, are not emancipated from their

180

hormones. Testosterone in men is critical for the maintenance of virility and potency.

7. The spinal cord contains the circuitry necessary for basic sexual reflexes. The preoptic area in males and the anterior and ventromedial hypothalamus in females regulate these reflexes. The activity of dopamine neurons facilitates male sexual behavior, and inhibits female sexual behavior. Serotonergic neurons depress sexual activity in males and females. The temporal lobe is especially important in the analysis of environmental circumstances appropriate for sexual activity.

8. Androgens are aromatized within the brain and converted to estrogen. Estrogen, when it enters cells within the male fetus, is responsible for androgenization. Alphafetoprotein, found in female fetuses, binds to estrogens, preventing them from entering cells and, thus, prevents a female fetus from being masculinized by estrogen.

Key Words

organizational effect (p. 316)

activational effect (p. 316)

sexually dimorphic (p. 316)

gametes (p. 317)

mitosis (p. 317)

meiosis (p. 318)

karyotype (p. 318)

differentiation (p. 320)

Müllerian system (p. 320)

Wolffian system (p. 320)

gonad (p. 320)

Müllerian-inhibiting substance (p. 321)

androgen (p. 321)

gonadotrophic releasing hormone (p. 323)

follicle-stimulating hormone (p. 323)

luteinizing hormone (p. 323)

estrogen (p. 323)

testosterone (p. 323)

hermaphrodite (p. 324)

estrous cycle (p. 326)

ovarian follicle (p. 326)

corpus luteum (p. 326)

gestagen (p. 326)

luteinizing hormone releasing hormone (p. 329)

intromission (p. 330)

Coolidge effect (p. 331)

lordosis (p. 332)

estradiol (p. 334)

androgenization (p. 336)

andrenogenital syndrome (p. 337)

Turner's syndrome (p. 339)

androgenic insensitivity syndrome (p. 340)

facultative homosexuality (p. 346)

medial forebrain bundle (p. 349)

preoptic area (p. 349)

aromatization (p. 353)

nonaromatizable androgen (p. 354)

alphafetoprotein (p. 355)

diethylstilbestrol (p. 356)

LEARNING OBJECTIVES FOR CHAPTER 11

When you have mastered the material in the chapter, you will
be able to:

1. Explain how chromosomes determine sex.

2. Describe the embryonic steps leading to genital dimorphism.

3. Describe the organizational effects of sex hormones on the brain and
   their involvement in the menstrual and estrous cycle.

4. Contrast the sexual behavior of male and female mammals.

5. Describe the organizational effects of sex hormones on sexual behavior.

6. Contrast the activational effects of sex hormones in females and males.

7. Discuss the hypotheses concerning possible biological causes of homosexuality.

8. Describe the spinal and brain mechanisms of sexual behavior in both
   human and non-human mammals.

9. Explain the biochemical mechanism underlying prenatal androgenization.

10. Describe how sex hormones can activate cells in the central nervous
    system.

OBJECTIVE 11-1: Explain how chromosomes determine sex.

---

1. List the steps that explain how the human ova, when fertilized, ends up
   with a full complement of 46 chromosomes. (p. 317)

2. Explain how the sex of the fertilized egg is determined at conception.
   (p. 319)

3. Below, on the left, are important terms associated with cell processes involved in fertilization. Match these terms with their best descriptions on the right. (pp. 317-319)

      ___ mitosis   a. cell division of gametes

      ___ karyotype   b. ova and sperm

      ___ meiosis   c. visualization of chromosomes

      ___ XX   d. chromosome complement of female

      ___ XY   e. cell division

      ___ gamete   f. chromosome complement of male

OBJECTIVE 11-2: Describe the embryonic steps leading to genital dimorphism.

---

4. List the steps, starting from undifferentiated bisexuality, that lead to the development of female gonads in the XX embryo. (pp. 320-323)

5. Do the same for the XY embryo. (pp. 320-323)

6. What are the effects of removing the gonads just after they are differentiated? Using your answer, explain why we say that "nature's impulse is to create a female". (p. 321)

7. Below, on the left, are important terms associated with embryonic sexual dimorphism. Match these terms with their best descriptions on the right. (pp. 320-323)

___ Müllerian system

___ Wolfian system

___ primordial gonad

___ Müllerian-inhibiting substance

___ androgen

a. "bisexual" gonads

b. causes regression of female internal genitalia

c. "male hormone"

d. precursor of female sex organs

e. precursor of male sex organs

8. Beginning at puberty, list the hormonal steps that result in sexual maturation. (p. 323)

Females   Males

9. Name four effects of estrogen on the female body and five effects of testosterone on the male body. (p. 323)

Estrogen:

a)

b)

c)

d)

Testosterone:

a)

b)

c)

d)

e)

10. Where is androstenedione produced? (p. 324) _____

    What role does this "male" hormone play in the development of female
    sexual characteristics? (p. 324)

11. Give two examples illustrating the fact that the bisexual potential of
    some secondary sex characteristics remains throughout life. (p. 324)

OBJECTIVE 11-3: Describe the organizational effects of sex hormones
                on the brain and their involvement in the menstrual
                and estrous cycle.

---

12. Differentiate between the organizational and activational effects of
    sex hormones. (pp. 316,325)

13. On the following page is a graph showing the flux in the hormones in-
    volved in the menstrual cycle. Label the figure, then explain how
    hormones produce periodic ovulation and menstruation. (pp. 326,327)

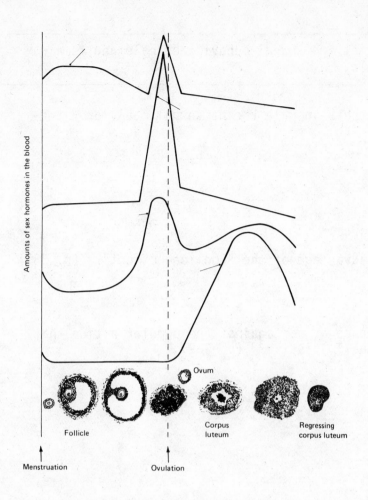

14. What accounts for cyclicity of pituitary hormone release in females? (p. 328)

15. Cite evidence that androgenization of the female hypothalamus can occur only during a critical period in development. (pp. 328,329)

16. Describe the microanatomical differences between male and female pre-optic areas. (p. 329)

```
┌─────────────────────────────────────────────────────────────────────┐
│    OBJECTIVE 11-4:  Contrast the sexual behavior of male and female   │
│                     mammals.                                          │
└─────────────────────────────────────────────────────────────────────┘
```

17. List the sequence of events in male rodent sexual behavior.
     (pp. 330,331)

18. What is the selective advantage of the "Coolidge effect"? (p. 331)

19. What experimental evidence argues against the popular notion that
     female animals are sexually passive? (p. 332)

```
┌─────────────────────────────────────────────────────────────────────┐
│    OBJECTIVE 11-5:  Describe the organizational effects of sex hormones│
│                     on sexual behavior.                               │
└─────────────────────────────────────────────────────────────────────┘
```

20. Diagram the biosynthesis of sex steroids. (p. 334)

21. Since all the sex steroids above are present in both males and females,
     what determines genital and behavioral dimorphism? (p. 334)

22. Below is a table summarizing the studies that show that sex hormones appropriate to the chromosomal sex of an animal must be present at an early critical period in order for gender-appropriate sexual behavior to occur in adulthood. Indicate, in the far right column, the effects of hormone treatment given at birth or in adulthood on sexual behavior. (pp. 335,336)

Sex	Hormones at birth	Hormones at adulthood	Sexual behavior
Male	Estrogen or no hormone treatment	Progesterone + estrogen Testosterone None	
	Testosterone	Progesterone + estrogen Testosterone None	
Female	Estrogen or no hormone treatment	Progesterone + estrogen Testosterone None	
	Testosterone	Progesterone + estrogen Testosterone None	

23. Describe the effects of prenatal androgenization in human females. What is the name of this syndrome? (pp. 336,337)

24. Compare the effects of early androgenization of humans, monkeys and other species. (p. 338)

189

25. Why does Turner's syndrome provide evidence that prenatal estrogen does not appear to be essential in producing a female? (p. 339)

26. How does the androgenic insensitivity syndrome once again demonstrate that "nature's impulse is to produce a female"? (pp. 339-341)

27. "Appropriate" sex roles in human beings seem to be powerfully influenced by socialization and learning. Give some clinical evidence to support this contention. (pp. 341,342)

```
┌─────────────────────────────────────────────────────────────────────┐
│   OBJECTIVE 11-6:  Contrast the activational effects of sex hormones  │
│                    in females and males.                             │
└─────────────────────────────────────────────────────────────────────┘
```

28. Contrast the hormonal control of sexual interest in species with menstrual cycles (primates) versus those with estrous cycles. (pp. 342-344)

29. Do variations in hormone levels during a female primate's menstrual cycle influence her libido? Explain. (p. 343)

30. What evidence suggests that a woman's sexual activity or desire is not dependent on estrogen? (p. 343)

31. Women and female rodents differ in their behavioral response to androgens. Explain. (p. 344)

32. What role does the adrenal gland play in sexual activity and desire? (pp. 344,345)

33. What arguments can be made against the popular idea that men are "emancipated from their hormones"? (p. 345)

```
OBJECTIVE 11-7:  Discuss the hypotheses concerning possible biologi-
                 cal causes of homosexuality.
```

34. Explain how sexual behavior of an adult female rat can be influenced by the number of her male siblings. (p. 346)

35. Many researchers have searched for a correlation between hormone levels and male and female homosexuality. What conclusions can you draw about the causes of human homosexuality? (pp. 346,347)

36. Explain how maternal stress can affect sexual behavior later in her male offspring. (pp. 346,347)

OBJECTIVE 11-8:   Describe the spinal and brain mechanisms of sexual
behavior in both human and non-human mammals.

37. Describe the kind, degree and experience of sexual activity following
transection of the cervical spinal cord in human and other mammals.
(pp. 347-349)

38. What is the role of the brain in relation to spinal sexual reflexes?
(p. 347)

39. What is the major neural pathway involved in penile erection? (p. 349)

40. Indicate the role of specific hypothalamic nuclei in male and female
sexual behavior in rats. (pp. 349,350)

41. Indicate the effects of specific monoaminergic agonists and antagonists
on sexual behavior. What conclusions can we draw about the role of
serotonin and dopamine in sexual behavior? (p. 350)

42. Discuss the clinical and experimental data that demonstrate an important role for the temporal lobe in sexual behavior. (pp. 351,352)

OBJECTIVE 11-9: Explain the biochemical mechanisms underlying androgenization.

43. Explain how aromatization of androgens is responsible for the masculin-ization of the male fetus. (pp. 352-354)

44. Indicate the effect of the treatments below on the masculinization or feminization of fetuses. (pp. 353,354)

a. testosterone _____

b. androstenedione _____

c. dihydrotestosterone _____

d. androsterone _____

e. estrogen antagonist _____

f. aromatization blocking drugs _____

What conclusion can you draw from the above results? (pp. 353-355)

45. If estrogen is the important agent in androgenization, why aren't female fetuses masculinized? (p. 355)

46. Explain in a diagram how alphafetoprotein deactivates estrogen in the female fetus. (pp. 354,355)

47. Using your diagram on the preceding page, explain why diethylstilbes-trol (DES) can masculinize female human fetuses. (pp. 355,356)

OBJECTIVE 11-10: Describe how sex hormones can activate cells in
the central nervous system.

---

48. How can autoradiography experiments tell us where steroid hormone receptors are located in the brain? (pp. 356,357)

49. Indicate where in the brain receptors are located for each of the fol-lowing sex hormones. (p. 357)

    a. estrogen _____

    b. testosterone _____

    c. progesterone _____

50. What happens to an animal's behavior when small quantities of steroid hormones are placed in specific brain regions? (p. 357)

Thought Questions

1. Throughout human history, it seems that wars have been initiated and fought by men (at least primarily). Do you think there might be a link between male hormones and some of the worst aspects of human culture?

2. Examine your own sexual preferences. Do you think they are the result of your genes, hormones and physical structure or your individual socia-lization?

12

Regulation and the Control of Food Intake

Essential Concepts

1. The necessity for a constant internal milieu in complex, multicellular, mobile organisms requires that the extracellular fluid be carefully maintained by both physiological and behavioral regulatory mechanisms.

2. The principal source of energy in almost all tissue is glucose. Energy can be derived from the breakdown of various substances: glycogen, fats and amino acids. Organisms can both store energy (absorptive phase) and convert stored substances into usable forms (fasting phase). The absorptive phase is characterized by the conversion of glucose into glycogen within liver and muscle, the synthesis of proteins from amino acids and the conversion of amino acids to fat for storage in adipose tissue. The fasting phase is characterized by the conversion of stored nutrients into glucose (for the brain), ketones (for all the body except the liver) and fatty acids (for all the body except the brain).

3. The nervous system and four hormones control the metabolic pathways that determine whether the organism is in the fasting or absorptive phase. Blood glucose levels, either directly or indirectly, control the secretion of these hormones and the activity of sympathetic fibers innervating the liver. Insulin, secreted by the pancreas, facilitates the entry of glucose into cells and increases the conversion of glucose to stored forms of energy. Glucagon, epinephrine and growth hormone stimulate the liver to convert stored nutrients into glucose and facilitate the breakdown of fats for energy. High levels of blood glucose stimulate insulin secretion, while the release of glucagon from the pancreas is facilitated by low blood glucose levels.

4. There are three principal sources of energy: glucose, fats and amino acids. These substances have each been suggested as the system variable monitored in the control of feeding behavior. The glucostatic theory suggests that the most important variable in feeding is glucose, and that cells sensitive to glucose availability control eating. The VMH was once believed to contain glucoreceptor cells that become active when

195

glucose availability is high and result in satiety. It has also been suggested that LH neurons respond to decreased glucose and stimulate feeding. Recent experiments have cast doubt on the role of brain gluco-receptors in the regulation of food intake and point to receptors in the liver as being important in food intake regulation through vagus nerve efferents to the brain. The lipostatic theory of feeding is supported by the fact that fat deposits are regulated; however, attempts to iden-tify system variables have not met with success. The aminostatic theory is supported by the fact that protein rich meals are very satiating but amino acid detectors appear to be located in the liver, not the brain.

5. Head factors, gastric and duodenal factors as well as liver factors work together to suppress feeding. Since VMH lesions cause obesity and LH lesions produce aphagia, these areas of the hypothalamus play a role in the neural mechanisms of feeding behavior. Some believe that VMH le-sions alter metabolism so that an animal is constantly in the absorptive phase. LH lesions may somehow alter the set point for body weight. The nigrostriatal dopaminergic bundle has been implicated in the LH syndrome. The ventral noradrenergic bundle, traveling near the VMH, has been shown to be involved in satiety.

Key Words

interstitial fluid (p. 360)

poikilotherm/homiotherm (p. 361)

system variable (p. 362)

set point (p. 362)

correctional mechanism (p. 362)

negative feedback (p. 363)

open system (p. 363)

pepsin (p. 366)

duodenum (p. 366)

cholecystokinin (p. 366)

hepatic portal system (p. 367)

bile (p. 367)

emulsification (p. 368)

absorptive phase (p. 369)

fasting phase (p. 369)

glycogen (p. 369)

adipose tissue (p. 369)

free fatty acids (p. 369)

ketones (p. 370)

insulin (p. 371)

pancreatic islet cells (p. 372)

diabetes mellitus (p. 372)

glucagon (p. 373)

glucostatic hypothesis (p. 375)

lipostatic hypothesis (p. 375)

aminostatic hypothesis (p. 375)

2-deoxyglucose (p. 375)

alloxan (p. 377)

hyperphagia (p. 377)

hypoglycemia (p. 380)

esophagotomy (p. 382)

pyloric sphincter (p. 386)

intraperitoneal injection (p. 389)

ventromedial nucleus (p. 397)

VMH obesity syndrome (p. 398)

dynamic phase (p. 398)

static phase (p. 398)

cephalic phase (p. 398)

ventral noradrenergic bundle (p. 399)

lateral hypothalamic syndrome (p. 402)

adipsia (p. 402)

aphagia (p. 402)

nigrostriatal bundle (p. 404)

LEARNING OBJECTIVES FOR CHAPTER 12

When you have mastered the material in the chapter, you will
be able to:

LESSON 1:   REGULATORY MECHANISMS, DIGESTION AND METABOLISM

1. Explain why the "free life" of multicellular organisms requires regu-
    latory mechanisms.

2. Describe all the components implicit in any regulatory system.

3. List the steps involved in the digestion of food.

4. Describe the biochemical events that occur during the absorptive and
    fasting phases.

5. Explain why insulin and glucagon are so important in the control of
    metabolism.

LESSON 2:   THE SEARCH FOR GLUCORECEPTORS, SYSTEM VARIABLES AND
            SATIETY MECHANISMS

6. Evaluate the importance of glucose and glucoreceptors in the control of
    hunger and eating.

7. Evaluate the importance of fats (lipids) and proteins (amino acids) in
    the control of food intake.

8. Evaluate the importance of GI receptors, from mouth to large intestine,
    in producing satiety.

9. Explain the role of the liver in the control of eating.

10. Summarize what we know about the role of the hypothalamus and associa-
    ted brain structures in hunger, satiety and metabolism.

LESSON 1:   REGULATORY MECHANISMS, DIGESTION AND METABOLISM

OBJECTIVE 12-1:   Explain why the "free life" of multicellular
                  organisms requires regulatory mechanisms.

---

1. List the regulatory mechanisms that we, as complex multicellular organ-
    isms, have developed in the "pursuit of a free life". (pp. 360,361)

2. Compare the regulatory demands of single celled organisms, poikilotherms and homiotherms. (p. 361)

OBJECTIVE 12-2: Describe all the components implicit in any regulatory system.

---

3. What are the four essential components of a regulatory system? (p. 362)

a. _____

b. _____

c. _____

d. _____

4. Give an original example of both negative and positive feedback. (p. 363)

5. On the following page is a diagram of O'Kelly's model of regulation. Explain each component of the model in terms of how the body regulates eating and hunger (satiety). (p. 363)

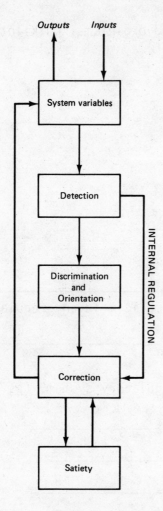

6. Describe the basic experimental procedures involved in answering each of the following questions about the regulatory process involved in food intake and satiety. (p. 364)

   a. What is the relevant system variable?

   b. Where in the body are the detectors for the system?

   c. What brain mechanisms control ingestive behavior?

7. Below is an ordered list of the major steps in the digestion of food.
    Indicate the function of each step and indicate the biochemical proces-
    ses that occur at each step. (pp. 365-368)

    a. Chewing and salivating.

    b. Swallowing chewed food into the stomach.

    c. Stomach churning and gastric secretion.

    d. Contents of stomach empty into the duodenum.

    e. Water-soluble nutrients enter capillaries of intestinal villi.

    f. Pancreas secretes insulin and glucagon into duodenum.

    g. Liver secretes bile into duodenum.

    h. Contents of small intestine pushed into large intestine.

8. Below, on the left, is a list of substances important in digestion.
    Next to each, indicate which organ secretes the substance and what its
    function is in the biochemistry of digestion. (pp. 366-368)

    a. pepsin

    b. cholecystokinin

c. bicarbonate

d. bile

OBJECTIVE 12-4: Describe the biochemical events that occur during
the absorptive and fasting phases.

---

9. What are the three types of nutrients absorbed into the body after a
balanced meal is eaten? (p. 369)

10. Describe what happens to glucose, amino acids and fats during the
absorptive phase. (p. 369)

11. The dominant characteristic of the absorptive phase is the storage of
energy. What is the dominant characteristic of the fasting phase?
(pp. 369,370)_____

12. List the metabolic events of the fasting phase. (pp. 370,371)

13. Below, on the left, is a list of important metabolic processes that
occur during either the absorptive or fasting phase. Indicate whether
each process is characteristic of the absorptive or fasting phase, and
in what tissue each process occurs. (pp. 369-371)

a. glucose → glycogen _____

b. fat → free fatty acid _____

c. glycogen → glucose _____

d. glucose → fat _____

e. amino acids → protein _____

f. glycerol → glucose _____

g. protein → amino acids _____

h. free fatty acid → ketones _____

i. amino acids → glucose _____

OBJECTIVE 12-5: Explain why insulin and glucagon are so important
in the control of metabolism.

---

14. Name the two hormones secreted by the pancreas that are involved in
metabolism. (pp. 371-373)

_____   _____

15. What is the cause of diabetes mellitus? (p. 372)

Explain why the urine of an untreated diabetic tastes sweet. (p. 372)

Why can diabetes mellitus, left untreated, lead to death? (p. 372)

16. What are the six metabolic effects of insulin? (pp. 372,373)

a. _____

b. _____

c. _____

d. _____

e. _____

f. _____

17. What three factors control insulin secretion? (p. 373)

18. What happens to pancreatic insulin release when blood glucose level is high? (p. 373)

19. Explain how low levels of insulin insure that metabolism enters the fasting phase. (p. 373)

20. What factor triggers pancreatic secretion of glucagon? (p. 373)

21. List the metabolic effects of glucagon during the fasting phase. (p. 373)

22. What are three other factors that operate during the fasting phase to enhance the breakdown of stored nutrients to usable energy? (pp. 373,374)

LESSON 2: THE SEARCH FOR GLUCORECEPTORS, SYSTEM VARIABLES AND
SATIETY MECHANISMS

OBJECTIVE 12-6: Evaluate the importance of glucose and glucoreceptors in the control of hunger and eating.

23. Explain why simply monitoring food (calorie) intake is not sufficient as a mechanism to regulate body weight. (p. 374)

24. Explain why the most important factors for eliciting hunger must be centrally located, while satiety could be produced by receptors in the digestive system. (p. 374)

25. Explain the logic underlying Jean Mayer's (1955) "glucose utilization" theory. (p. 375)

26. How do the effects of systemic and brain ventricle injections of 2-deoxyglucose support Mayer's hypothesis? (pp. 375,376)

27. Explain why one would not expect "glucose availability receptors" to be found in the brain. (p. 376)

28. Cite evidence that demonstrates the unimportance of brain glucoreceptors in the control of hunger. (pp. 376,377)

OBJECTIVE 12-7: Evaluate the importance of fats (lipids) and proteins (amino acids) in the control of food intake.

29. Give the rationale for the hypothesis that the amount of fat deposits may be an important factor in long-term control of food intake and body weight. (p. 377)

30. Explain how rats are made experimentally diabetic. (p. 377)

What happens to food intake following this procedure? (p. 377)

Why are lipids the principal fuel in diabetic animals? (pp. 377,378)

31. Explain the steps that Friedman (1978) used with diabetic rats to demonstrate that food intake is modulated by available calories, whether they are in the form of carbohydrates or lipids. (pp. 378,379)

32. Describe the experiment by Liebelt, Bordelon and Liebelt (1973) that shows that the amount of fat in the body is regulated. (pp. 379,380)

33. What are essential amino acids? (p. 380)

34. Explain why protein is an essential component of our diet. (p. 380)

35. Explain the metabolic rationale behind high-protein reducing diets. (p. 380)

36. Give some evidence that blood level of amino acids is a major system variable that regulates food intake. (pp. 380,381)

37. Why would we predict that diabetic rats would not respond to the reduction of protein content in their diet by increasing their food intake? (p. 381)

OBJECTIVE 12-8: Evaluate the importance of GI receptors, from mouth to large intestine, in producing satiety.

---

38. Describe some effects of positive feedback from "head factors" on eating. (pp. 381,382)

39. Explain how experimental esophagotomy has demonstrated the independent importance of head factors in satiety. (pp. 382,383)

40. Cite some evidence that the stomach is not very important in regulating food intake. (p. 383)

41. Cite some evidence that it does, under special circumstances. (p. 383)

42. Several experiments during the last decade have demonstrated that food substances injected directly into the stomach or duodenum can, under some circumstances, produce satiety. More recently, however, evidence has emerged suggesting that satiety can occur through stomach or duodenum injection only when the nutrient is in a physiologically appropriate form (i.e., partially digested). Describe the experiments upon which this conclusion is based. (pp. 383-386)

43. Describe the "pyloric cuff" experiments by Deutsch and his colleagues. (pp. 387,388)

44. What hypothesis did Deutsch (1978) propose to account for the fact that the stomach signals satiety only when it is full of nutrients? (p. 388)

OBJECTIVE 12-9: Explain the role of the liver in the control of eating.

---

45. Describe the two experiments by Russek that suggested that the liver contains glucoreceptors. (p. 389)

46. What happened when Russek and his colleagues (1963) blocked conduction in the vagus nerve connecting the liver to the brain? What is the significance of this finding? (pp. 389,390)

47. What electrophysiological evidence argues that the liver contains glucoreceptors that are important in food regulation? (p. 390)

48. Explain Russek and Racotta's (1979) hypothesized mechanism concerning the system variables monitored by liver receptors. (pp. 390,391)

49. Give four pieces of evidence that support their hypothesis. (p. 391)

50. Explain why the following experimental results further substantiate the importance of liver receptors and not brain receptors in the regulation of eating. (pp. 392,393)

    a. 2-DG injected directly into the hepatic portal vein produces large increases in food intake.

    b. Injections of glucose, fructose or mannose all produce satiety.

    c. Injections of ketone do not produce satiety.

51. Describe the experiment that showed that brain receptors control the release of epinephrine by the adrenal glands in response to its own need for glucose. (p. 394)

52. Explain how Granneman and Friedman's (1978) study showed that the brain contains receptors that can stimulate hunger even in the absence of information from the liver, while the liver contains receptors that can produce both hunger and satiety. (p. 394)

```
OBJECTIVE 12-10:  Summarize what we know about the role of the
                  hypothalamus and associated brain structures in
                  hunger, satiety and metabolism.
```

53. Describe the two stages of the ventromedial hypothalamic obesity syndrome. (p. 398)

54. What evidence supports Powley's (1977) "cephalic phase" hypothesis of the VMH syndrome? (p. 398)

55. Evaluate the notion that the VMH is a "satiety center". (pp. 398,399)

56. How did Gold (1973) demonstrate the importance of the ventral noradrenergic bundle in the VMH obesity syndrome? (p. 399)

57. A more recent study by Gold's group (1977) used the "knife-cut" technique to demonstrate the importance of the paraventricular hypothalamic nucleus in eating and satiety. Describe, in a drawing, the relevant fiber system. (pp. 399,400)

58. Evaluate the hypothesis that the vagus nerve mediates the VMH obesity syndrome. (pp. 400,401)

59. Evaluate the hypothesis that hyperinsulinemia mediates the VMH obesity syndrome. (p. 401)

60. What is Friedman and Stricker's (1976) explanation for the VMH obesity syndrome? (p. 401)

61. What parallels does Schachter (1971) see between obesity in humans and the VMH obesity syndrome? (pp. 401,402)

62. How might human obesity be related to stress? Give some experimental evidence. (p. 402)

63. Describe the lateral hypothalamic syndrome. (p. 402)

64. How does Teitelbaum (1971) explain the recovery of eating observed in carefully nursed lateral hypothalamic animals? (pp. 402,403)

65. What evidence supports Powley and Keesey's (1970) hypothesis that LH lesions produce a new set point for body weight? (pp. 402,403)

66. How are the LH syndrome and the nigrostriatal dopamine system inter-related? (p. 404)

67. In summary, how would you answer the question of whether the lateral hypothalamus is a "feeding center"? (pp. 404,405)

Thought Question

1. If someone were to ask you, as a student of physiological psychology, why some people are overweight while others are not, what would be your answer to this complex question?

13

Thirst and the Control of Mineral Intake

Essential Concepts

1. Reabsorption of salt and water by the kidneys and the consumption of
    water by an organism maintain the osmotic balance of the body tissues.
    The balance between the osmotic pressure of the extracellular fluid
    and the intracellular fluid must be carefully regulated for normal
    biochemical functioning of tissues.

2. The nephrons of the kidneys extract fluid from the blood while
    reabsorption of fluid by means of active and passive processes occurs
    in the renal tubules. Sodium is actively reabsorbed against its
    concentration gradient and water consequently reenters capillaries in
    a passive fashion, following its concentration gradient.

3. The rate of sodium reabsorption in the kidneys is enhanced by the hormone
    aldosterone, which is secreted by the adrenal glands. The secretion of
    aldosterone is stimulated by angiotensin, a substance produced by the
    secretion of renin from the kidneys. Renin is released in response to
    neural stimulation or to decreased renal blood flow. Water reabsorption
    by the renal tubules is controlled by antidiuretic hormone which is
    produced in the supraoptic nucleus of the hypothalamus and released by
    the posterior pituitary gland. Diabetes insipidus results from a
    deficiency of antidiuretic hormone.

4. A fall in venous blood pressure is detected by baroreceptors in the left
    atrium of the heart and triggers secretion of antidiuretic hormone and
    the production of angiotensin. A decreased arterial blood flow to the
    kidneys will also result in production of angiotensin.

5. Thirst and the resulting drinking are able to restore and maintain fluid
    balance. Restricted blood flow to the kidneys and constriction of the
    vena cava also result in what is called extracellular or volumetric
    thirst. Osmometric thirst results from either increased osmotic
    pressure of the extracellular fluid or the ensuing loss of intracellular
    fluid.

214

6. Angiotensin-sensitive neurons are located in hypothalamic regions bordering on the ventricular system. These areas, the subfornical organ and the organum vasculosum of the lamina terminalis, are involved in volumetic thirst. Osmoreceptors in the medial preoptic area are important in producing osmometric thirst. The nucleus circularis, a specific sensory area near the walls of the third ventricle, appears to regulate the secretion of aldosterone. Two efferent pathways of the lateral hypothalamus appear to be involved in the motor control of drinking; 1) a lateral pathway from the LH terminating in the ventral tegmental area and 2) a more medial pathway terminating in the periaqueductal gray of the midbrain.

7. An animal that is deprived of sodium will develop a "sodium appetite"; an immediate preference for sodium over other minerals. Animals seem to have an innate capacity to recognize sodium and will regulate their intake as the body demands. Natural selection has produced an elegant mechanism for the regulation of other vital substances. If the regular diet of an animal lacks an essential ingredient, a conditioned aversion to that specific diet develops. If the ingestion of a new food is followed by recovery from illness that food is subsequently preferred.

Key Terms

iso-osmotic (p. 409)

hydrostatic pressure (p. 409)

osmotic pressure (p. 409)

isotonic (p. 411)

nephron (p. 411)

urethra (p. 411)

glomerulus (p. 411)

Bowman's capsule (p. 411)

renal tubule (p. 411)

aldosterone (p. 414)

renin (p. 414)

juxtoglomerular cell (p. 414)

angiotensin (p. 414)

antidiuretic hormone (ADH) (p. 415)

diabetes insipidus (p. 415)

hypovolemia (p. 417)

baroreceptor (p. 417)

volumetric thirst (p. 419)

polyethylene glycol (p. 419)

nephrectomy (p. 420)

osmometric thirst (p. 421)

Saralasin (p. 425)

subfornical organ (SFO) (p. 426, 427)

organum vasculosum of the lamina terminalis (OVLT) (p. 427)

nucleus circularis (p. 430)

ventral tegmental area (p. 432)

periaqueductal gray (p. 432)

sodium appetite (p. 414, 434)

neophobia (p. 435)

conditioned aversion (p. 435)

LEARNING OBJECTIVES FOR CHAPTER 13

When you have mastered the material in the chapter, you will be able to:

1. Describe the physical forces and physiological mechanisms involved in the formation and circulation of interstitial fluid.

2. Explain why and how urine is produced by the kidneys.

3. Describe the physiological and hormonal mechanisms that regulate sodium retention and water reabsorption within the kidney.

4. Explain how hypo- and hypervolemia can occur and the physiological mechanisms that operate to correct for these conditions.

5. Explain why the restoration of proper extra- and intracellular fluid balance requires ingestive behavior (thirst and drinking) and receptors responsive to intracellular fluid volume.

6. Describe the physiological events responsible for the satiation of thirst.

7. Describe the behavioral mechanisms which insure that animals ingest an amount of water that is closely related to the osmotic demand of a meal.

8. Discuss the role of the subfornical organ and the organum vasculosum of the lamina terminalis in angiotensin-produced (volumetric) thirst.

9. Summarize what we know about the location and functioning of hypothalamic receptors responsible for osmometric thirst.

10. Describe the neural pathways involved in the motor control of drinking that is caused by angiotensin and osmotic conditions.

11. Explain why we believe that sodium appetite and sodium recognition are innate behavioral mechanisms and not learned.

12. Explain how the behavioral mechanism of conditioned aversion helps to regulate the intake of vital minerals and vitamins.

OBJECTIVE 13-1: Describe the physical forces and the physiological mechanisms involved in the formation and circulation of interstitial fluid.

---

1. Explain how hydrostatic and osmotic pressure result in just the right volume and ion concentration of interstitial fluid. (p. 409)

2. The diagram below shows the process of plasma filtration within capillaries. Explain how the forces at the arterial and venous ends of capillaries perfectly balance. (pp. 409-410)

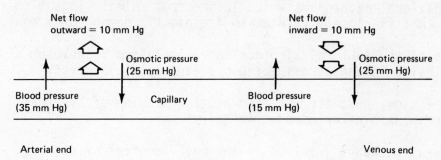

3. Name the three fluid compartments of the body and indicate the percent of total body water of each. (p. 410)

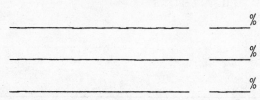

4. Explain how these fluid compartments are interdependent. (pp. 410-411)

OBJECTIVE 13-2: Explain why and how urine is produced by the kidneys.

---

5. Draw a diagram showing the anatomy of the kidney and the route by which urine is formed and passed to the outside of the body. (p. 411)

6. Describe the active process by which NaCl is reabsorbed within renal tubules. (p. 411)

7. Explain how water is passively reabsorbed within the renal tubule. (p. 411-412)

OBJECTIVE 13-3: Describe the physiological and hormonal mechanisms that regulate sodium retention and water reabsorption within the kidney.

8. Control of water and sodium balance is achieved by 1) altering the

   _____ of sodium transport and 2) varying the _____

   of the walls of the renal tubules and collecting ducts. (p. 413)

9. Why does a sodium deficit result in the loss of water by the body? (p. 413)

10. What hormone regulates the reabsorption of sodium? (p. 414)

    _____

11. Why will damage to the adrenal glands cause a sodium appetite? (p. 414)

12. Explain how the rate of aldosterone secretion from the adrenals is controlled. (p. 414)

13. Explain why reduction in either renal blood flow or increased activity of sympathetic efferents to the kidney causes sodium to be retained by the body. (p. 414)

14. Describe the synthesis and release of antidiuretic hormone and how it works to control the permeability of renal tubules to water. (p. 415)

15. What is the name of the disease caused by lack of ADH? _____
    What causes the symptoms of this disease? (p. 415)

```
OBJECTIVE 13-4:  Explain how hypo- and hypervolemia can occur and the
                 physiological mechansisms that operate to correct for
                 these conditions.
```

16. Define hypovolemia. (p. 417)

17. Loss of extracellular fluid results in the activiation of mechanisms that conserve the body's supply of water and sodium. Next to each term below indicate the role of each in regulating extracellular fluid and correcting a hypervolemic condition. (p. 417)

    venous blood pressure

    baroreceptors

antidiuretic hormone

renin

renal blood flow

18. Explain why an injection of hypertonic saline causes a loss of intra-cellular fluid and. hence, hypervolemia. (p. 418)

19. List the events in the body which act to re-establish extracellular fluid balance following an injection of hypertonic saline. (p. 418)


```
OBJECTIVE 13-5:  Explain why the restoration of proper extra- and
                 intracellular fluid balance requires ingestive
                 behavior (thirst and drinking) and receptors
                 responsive to intracellular volume.
```


20. Why does the injection of colloids into the peritoneal cavity produce hypovolemia and thirst? (p. 419)

21. Explain why an injection of polyethylene glycol into the peritoneal cavity of rats, followed by drainage of the fluid, will produce a sodium deficiency. (p. 419)

22. Why did occlusion of the vena cava in Fitzsimons' experiment produce drinking in rats? (p. 420)

23. Below is a schematic representation of Fitzsimons' renal blood flow experiments. Explain why each procedure affected thirst in the way it did. What conclusions can we draw from this set of experiments? (p. 420)

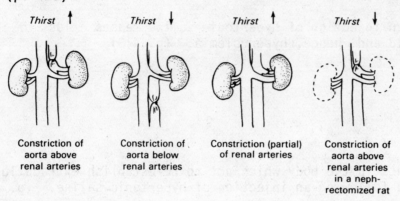

Thirst ↑	*Thirst* ↓	*Thirst* ↑	*Thirst* ↓
Constriction of aorta above renal arteries	Constriction of aorta below renal arteries	Constriction (partial) of renal arteries	Constriction of aorta above renal arteries in a neph-rectomized rat

24. How did Stricker (1973) show that both baroreceptors and renal blood flow detectors have an independent role in thirst produced by reduction in extracellular fluid? (pp. 420-421)

25. How is osmometric thirst different from volumetric thirst? (p. 421)

26. Describe the experimental evidence that indicates that cell shrinkage, and not increased osmotic pressure of extracellular fluid, is responsible for producing osmometric thirst. (p. 421)

27. What is the important difference between hypertonic solutions that produce drinking and those which do not? (pp. 421-422)

28. Diagram or list the series of events that lead to drinking after injection of a thirst-producing hypertonic solution. (pp. 421-422)

29. What evidence suggests that there are osmoreceptive cells residing within the brain? (p. 422)

OBJECTIVE 13-6: Describe the physiological events responsible for the satiation of thirst.

30. Which of the following signals thirst and which inhibits thirst? (p. 423)

cellular overhydration _____

hypovolemia _____

31. Explain how volumetric and osmometric dehydration work together to produce thirst. (p. 423)

OBJECTIVE 13-7: Describe the behavioral mechanisms which insure that animals ingest an amount of water that is closely related to the osmotic demand of a meal.

32. Why does the consumption of a meal produce a certain degree of hypervolemia? (p. 424)

33. How did Fitzsimons and Le Magnen (1969) show that the matching of water intake to water need during a meal is learned? (p. 424)

34. Describe an oral mechanism that might be involved in anticipatory drinking. (p. 424)

OBJECTIVE 13-8: Discuss the role of the subfornical organ and the organum vasculosum of the lamina terminalis in angiotensin-produced (volumetric) thirst.

35. What is the logic underlying the assertion that either renin or angiotensin acts on some class of brain cells to produce thirst? (p. 425)

36. What evidence is there that angiotensin is a stimulus for thirst and drinking? (p. 425)

37. How does angiotensin affect blood pressure? _____
How does Stricker (1977, 1978) explain the fact that angiotensin has a
somewhat paradoxical effect; it increases blood pressure and induces
drinking? (p. 425)

38. Stricker has hypothesized that the real role of angiotensin is to
maintain blood pressure despite _____.
(p. 425)

List the experimental evidence against this hypothesis. (p. 425)

39. Cite the evidence for the conclusion that both the subfornical organ
(SFO) and the organum vasculosum of the lamina terminalis (OVLT) are
sensitive to the hormone angiotensin. (p. 427)

40. Cite the evidence that suggests that the OVLT may be more important
than the SFO in eliciting drinking. (p. 427)

41. How did Brody and Johnson (1980) show that angiotensin-sensitive
neurons are located in the vicinity of the anteroventral third
ventricle? (p. 428)

OBJECTIVE 13-9:   Summarize what we know about the location and
                  functioning of hypothalamic receptors responsible for
                  osmometric thirst.

42. Why do we believe that the receptors involved in producing osmometric
     thirst are extracellular saline detectors? (p. 429)

43. There is evidence that the hypothalamus contains cells that are
     sensitive to angiotensin and other neurons thought to be osmoreceptors.
     What evidence suggests that there are osmoreceptors in the hypothalamus?
     (p. 430)

44. Name two areas of the hypothalamus thought to contain osmoreceptors.

     _____   _____

     Give experimental evidence in support of each area containing
     osmoreceptors. (p. 430)

45. Hatton (1976) has suggested that the nucleus circularis of the hypo-
     thalamus may be a specific locus of osmoreceptors.

     a. Describe the anatomy of this nucleus and its cells' relationship
        to surrounding capillaries. (p. 430)

     b. Give evidence from lesion studies that the nucleus circularis is
         involved in ADH release. (pp. 430-431)

c. What is the result of electrically stimulating the nucleus circularis? (p. 431)

d. What microanatomical changes occur in the cells of this nucleus during water deprivation? What is the significance of this change? (p. 431)

> OBJECTIVE 13-10: Describe the neural pathways involved in the motor control of drinking that is caused by angiotensin and osmotic conditions.

46. List the brain structures that have been implicated in the neural control of drinking. Indicate the possible function of each. (pp. 431-433)

47. Look at Figure 13-18. Describe the two efferent pathways of the lateral hypothalamus thought to be involved in the motor control of drinking. (p. 432)

48. What are the most recent hypotheses regarding the separate functions of the two pathways descending from the lateral hypothalamus to the ventral tegmental area and the periaqueductal gray? (pp. 432-433)

```
┌─────────────────────────────────────────────────────────────────────┐
│ OBJECTIVE 13-11:  Explain why we believe that sodium appetite and    │
│                   sodium recognition are innate behavioral mechanisms│
│                   and not learned.                                   │
└─────────────────────────────────────────────────────────────────────┘
```

49. Cite two experiments that demonstrate that sodium recognition is innate in rats. (p. 434)

50. Why does Stricker (1980) beleive that the brain contains receptors that are responsible for sodium appetite and are different from the receptors that mediate volumetric thirst? (pp. 434-435)

```
┌─────────────────────────────────────────────────────────────────────┐
│ OBJECTIVE 13-12:  Explain how the behavioral mechanism of conditioned│
│                   aversion helps to regulate the intake of vital     │
│                   minerals and vitamins.                             │
└─────────────────────────────────────────────────────────────────────┘
```

51. How is conditioned aversion produced? (pp. 435-436)

52. Explain how we know that it is that taste of a novel substance that is involved in conditioned aversion? (p. 436)

53. How does conditioned aversion explain why rats can learn to consume selectively diets that provide minerals or vitamins in which the animal is deficient? (pp. 436-437)

54. What experimental evidence supports the notion that rats can learn a positive association between diets and restitution of needed vitamins and minerals? (p. 437)

Thought Question

1. Is there any way to study independently the physiological mechanisms of thirst as opposed to drinking in experimental animals?

14

The Nature and Functions of Sleep

Essential Concepts

1. There are two distinct stages of sleep. Slow wave sleep (S sleep) is is characterized by a high voltage, low frequency synchronized EEG. Deep sleep (D sleep) is characterized by a low voltage, high frequency desynchronized EEG, loss of muscle tonus, rapid eye movements, PGO waves and the occurrence of dreaming. During an average night's sleep, periods of D sleep are separated by approximately 90 minutes of S sleep.

2. Is sleep a necessary biological function? Apparently not. Prolonged sleep deprivation in psychologically stable humans has no serious detrimental effect, although the urge to sleep is insistent and persistent. More highly evolved species engage in more D sleep than lower forms and human infants spend a higher proportion of sleep time in D sleep than adults. These facts have led to the suggestion that D sleep has important neural functions in the complex and developing brain.

3. The functions of S and D sleep have been studied by selectively depriving humans and other animals of stage 4 of S sleep or D sleep. The fact that D sleep deprivation one night leads to greater amounts of time spent in D sleep the next night (rebound phenomenon) has suggested that this form of sleep has an important biological function.

4. Growth hormone secretion is associated with S sleep and increased protein synthesis occurs during D sleep, suggesting that sleep has an important repair function. D sleep seems important for learning as well. Animals deprived of D sleep learn more slowly and new learning experiences increase subsequent D sleep time. From evidence available thus far, S sleep appears to be associated with bodily rest.

5. Various forms of sleep pathology related to D sleep have been observed in humans. The symptoms of narcolepsy may include sudden sleep attacks, cataplexy, sleep paralysis and hypnogogic hallucinations. Problems associated with S sleep include nocturnal enuresis, somnambulism and

night terrors. Sleep apnea, a form of insomnia, has been linked to sudden infant death syndrome in infants.

Key Terms

alpha activity (p. 440)

beta activity (p. 440)

delta activity (p. 441)

synchrony/desynchrony (p. 441)

electro-oculogram (p. 443)

REM sleep (p. 444)

paradoxical sleep (p. 444)

S sleep (p. 444)

D sleep (p. 444)

microsleep (p. 452)

delta sleep-inducing peptide (p. 453)

push-pull cannula (p. 454)

Ringer's solution (p. 454)

PGO waves (p. 459)

flower pot technique (p. 460)

sleep apnea (p. 465)

sudden infant death syndrome (p. 466)

narcolepsy (p. 466)

hypersomnia (p. 466)

cataplexy (p. 466)

sleep paralysis (p. 467)

hypnogogic hallucinations (p. 467)

nocturnal enuresis (p. 468)

somnambulism (p. 468)

night terrors (p. 468)

LEARNING OBJECTIVES FOR CHAPTER 14

When you have mastered the material in this chapter you will
be able to:

1. Explain the significance of synchrony and desynchrony of the EEG in
   relation to the states of consciousness - from alert wakefulness to
   deep sleep.

2. Describe the sequence of bodily and brain events that occur during a
   typical night's sleep.

3. Contrast the psychological, behavioral and physiological characteristics
   of S and D sleep.

4. Discuss the ontogeny and phylogeny of sleep.

5. Discuss the question of the biological necessity for D sleep in light of
   sleep deprivation studies in humans and other animals.

6. Describe the biochemical antecedents, concomitants and consequences of
   sleep.

7. Describe the effects of D sleep deprivation in both humans and experimental animals.

8. Contrast the two general theories that attempt to explain why we sleep:
   1) sleep as biological repair and 2) sleep as an adaptive response.

9. Describe the symptoms and possible causes of the following sleep
   pathologies and anomalies: insomnia, sleep apnea, sudden infant death
   syndrome, narcolepsy, hypersomnia, cataplexy, sleep paralysis,
   hypnogogic hallucinations, somnambulism and night terrors.

OBJECTIVE 14-1:   Explain the significance of synchrony and desynchrony
                  of the EEG in relation to the states of consciousness -
                  from alert wakefulness to deep sleep.

---

1. Draw and characterize the three major subdivisions of electroencephalo-
   graphic activity: alpha, beta and delta activity. (pp. 440-442)

2. Below are EEG records from various stages of wakefulness and sleep. Indicate from which state of consciousness these EEGs come and how you make your decision. (pp. 441-442)

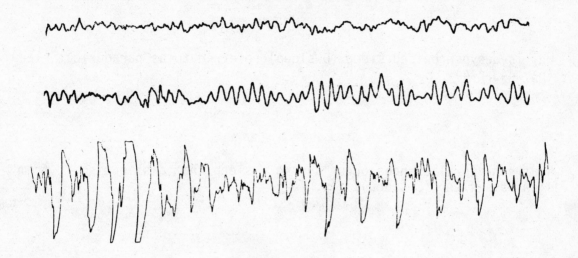

3. Explain, in terms of the electrical properties of neurons, the significance of a synchronous versus desynchronous EEG pattern. (p. 441)

OBJECTIVE 14-2: Describe the sequence of bodily and brain events that occur during a typical night's sleep.

4. Summarize the changes in the EEG during the first four stages of sleep. (p. 443)

5. Is the progression from the waking state to the sleeping state gradual? How has this question been answered experimentally? (p. 443)

6. Why is desynchronized sleep (D sleep) referred to as paradoxical sleep? (pp. 443-444)

7. What behavioral changes occur during D sleep that distinguish it from slow wave sleep (S sleep)? (p. 444)

8. The figure below depicts the typical pattern of sleep stages during a single night. Using this graph, describe the cycles of D sleep in terms of the EEG and the electro-oculogram (EOG). (p. 444)

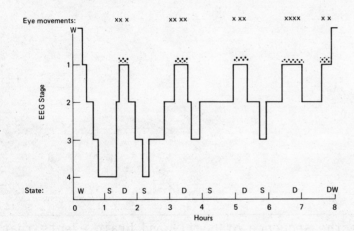

Figure from Hartmann, E., THE BIOLOGY OF DREAMING, 1967. Courtesy of Charles C. Thomas, Publisher, Springfield, Illinois.

9. What aspect of the sleep cycle suggests that there are intrinsic brain mechanisms that alternately produce S and D sleep? (p. 445)

```
┌─────────────────────────────────────────────────────────────────┐
│    OBJECTIVE 14-3:  Contrast the psychological, behavioral and physio- │
│                     logical characteristics of S and D sleep.     │
└─────────────────────────────────────────────────────────────────┘
```

10. List the physiological changes that occur in both the nervous system
    and the peripheral body during D sleep. (pp. 445-446)

11. How did Dement and his colleagues discover that eye movements during
    D sleep are directly related to the visual content of dreams? (pp.
    445-446)

12. What is the correspondence between real clock time and dream length?
    (p. 446)

13. When are penile erections most likely to occur during a night's sleep?
    (pp. 446-447)

    _____

14. Although most dreaming occurs during D sleep, S sleep is not devoid
    of mental activity. Contrast the "dreams" that occur during S and D
    sleep. (pp. 448-449)

15.   Explain why the ontogeny of sleep in humans contradicts the biological generalization that "ontogeny recapitulates phylogeny". (p. 449)

16.   What facts support the hypothesis that D sleep facilitates neural growth in postnatal mammals with immature nervous systems? (p. 449)

17.   How do we experimentally answer the question of whether sleep is a necessary biological function? (p. 450)

18.   It is a common belief that prolonged sleep deprivation can lead to personality disorders. Cite two pieces of evidence that support this view. (pp. 450-451)

Now give evidence that this view is incorrect. (p. 451)

What conclusions can you draw about the relation between sleep deprivation and personality disorder? (p. 451)


```
┌─────────────────────────────────────────────────────────────────────┐
│  OBJECTIVE 14-6:  Describe the biochemical antecedents, concomitants │
│                   and consequences of sleep.                        │
└─────────────────────────────────────────────────────────────────────┘
```


19. Explain how the delta sleep-inducing peptide was discovered. (pp. 452-453)

20. Give two pieces of evidence that this peptide does not play a crucial role in sleep. (p. 453)

21. What conclusion can be drawn regarding possible sleep and arousal-inducing chemical factors within the cerebrospinal fluid? (pp. 453-454)

22. What is the rationale for "push-pull cannula" experiments? (p. 454)

23. Evaluate the experiments conducted by Drucker-Colin's group using a push-pull cannula in cats. Do various brain regions contain sleep- and arousal-promoting biochemical substances? (pp. 454-455)

24. Growth hormone has been hypothesized to be causally related to S sleep. Using the graph below, explain the relation between sleep stage and plasma levels of growth hormone. (pp. 456-457)

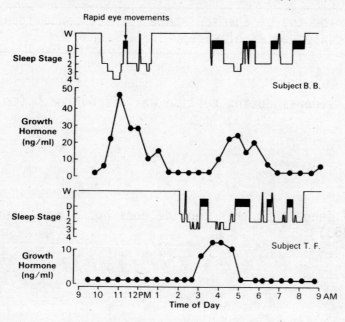

25. What evidence prevents us from concluding that the function of sleep is to provide a state in which growth hormone is secreted? (p. 457)

26. Cite the evidence that a function of D sleep is to facilitate protein repair of the brain. (pp. 457, 458)

OBJECTIVE 14-7: Describe the effects of D sleep deprivation in both humans and experimental animals.

---

27. How can we deprive a person of D sleep only? (p. 458)

28. What is the rebound phenomenon? (pp. 458-459)

29. What are PGO waves? (p. 459)
    brief phasic bursts of electrical activity found in the Pons, lateral Geniculate nucleus, and visual (Occipital) cortex seen in the D sleep of many animals.

30. When animals and humans are deprived of D sleep, which of the D sleep phenomenon will "escape" into S sleep? (p. 459)

239

31. Although D sleep deprivation is not necessarily detrimental to psychological health, some subtle emotional changes occur. What are these changes? (pp. 459-460)

32. Explain how the use of the "flower pot technigue" selectively deprives mice of D sleep. (p. 460)

33. The graph below shows the effects of either D or total sleep deprivation on maze learning in mice (Rideout, 1979). Explain the results and conclusions from this experiment using the data in the figure. (pp. 461-462)

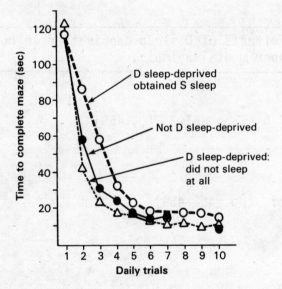

34. What data led to the suggestion that learning increases subsequent D sleep? (p. 462)

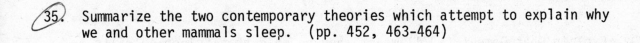

OBJECTIVE 14-8: Contrast the two general theories that attempt to
                explain why we sleep: 1) sleep as biological repair
                and 2) sleep as an adaptive response.

35. Summarize the two contemporary theories which attempt to explain why
    we and other mammals sleep. (pp. 452, 463-464)

36. Explain why growth hormone secretion and increased protein synthesis
    during sleep are evidence for the "sleep as biological repair"
    hypothesis. (pp. 456-458)

37. What is the argument and evidence for the hypothesis that sleep is an
    adaptive mechanism selected by the pressures of predation? (p. 463)

38. Give the pros and cons for the notion that we, as civilized animals,
    could theoretically dispense with sleep altogether. (p. 464)

```
┌─────────────────────────────────────────────────────────────────────┐
│  OBJECTIVE 14-9:   Describe the symptoms and possible causes of the   │
│                    following sleep pathologies and anomalies: insomnia,│
│                    sleep apnea, sudden infant death syndrome, narcolepsy,│
│                    hypersomnia, cataplexy, sleep paralysis, hypnogogic │
│                    hallucinations, somnambulism amd night terrors.    │
└─────────────────────────────────────────────────────────────────────┘
```

39. Explain what Dement (1974) meant when he said that "sleeping pills cause insomnia". (p. 465)

40. There are two types of insomnia; 1)pseudoinsomnia and 2) sleep apnea. Describe each. (p. 465)

41. What is the hypothesized link between sudden infant death syndrome and sleep apnea? Cite the evidence. (p. 466)

42. Differentiate narcolepsy from hypersomnia. (p. 466)

43. Describe the following symptoms of narcolepsy: a)narcoleptic sleep attacks and b)cataplexy. (p. 466)

44. What is believed to be the physiological basis of cataplexic attacks? (p. 467)

45. What are the characteristics and possible causes of sleep paralysis? (p. 467)

46. What different drugs have been used to treat narcolepsy versus D sleep disorders of cataplexy, sleep paralysis and hypnogogic hallucinations? (p. 468)

47. Name and describe three problems associated with S sleep in some individuals. (pp. 468-469)

15

Neural Mechanisms of the Sleep-Waking Cycle

Essential Concepts

1. The suprachiasmatic nucleus of the hypothalamus appears to serve as a biological clock responsible for circadian rhythms in many mammals. Some researchers have argued that neurons involved in biological rhythms use the process of protein synthesis as a time base.

2. Sleep is an active physiological process, not the result of neural fatigue. Early investigations into the neural mechanisms responsible for the sleep-waking cycle revealed that there is a rostral pontine region that is involved in maintaining wakefulness and a caudal pontine area actively responsible for sleep. The reticular formation plays an important role in arousal caused by sensory stimuli.

3. A noradrenergic system arising from the locus coeruleus in the pons also plays an active role in arousal. The most important sleep-producing region of the brainstem is the raphe, the destruction of which leads to insomnia. The raphe contains serotonergic neurons, suggesting serotonergic mediation of sleep. The nucleus of the solitary tract has a sleep-promoting effect when it is active.

4. It is the pons that contains mechanisms responsible for the initiation and regulation of D sleep. Cholinergic neurons of the central pons play a role in initiating or facilitating D sleep. Descending noradrenergic efferents of the locus coeruleus may inhibit muscular movements during D sleep. Ascending noradrenergic efferents of the locus coeruleus may inhibit the initiation of sleep. Serotonergic neurons of the dorsal raphe may restrict the phasic components of D sleep to the appropriate time. The executive mechanism for D sleep appears to lie caudal to the rostral pons, but probably within the pons itself.

5. The fact that animals with a cerveau isolé transection are eventually capable of periodic wakefulness induced investigators to search for a forebrain waking mechanism. Lesions of the posterior hypothalamus result in somnolence, but since the lesion-induced inactivity is often

accompanied by EEG desynchrony, it seems likely that these lesions interrupt motor systems involved in voluntary movement. The preoptic-basal forebrain region may be part of a forebrain sleep mechanism. Destruction of this region produces insomnia, while electrical stimulation of the preoptic area produces cortical synchrony.

Key Words

circadian rhythm (p. 471)

Zeitgeber (p. 473)

suprachiasmatic nucleus (SCN) (p. 474)

midcollicular transection (p. 479)

cerveau isolé (pp. 479-480)

encéphale isolé (p. 480)

midpontine pretrigeminal transection (p. 481)

locus coeruleus (p. 485)

raphe (p. 486)

nucleus of the solitary tract (p. 486)

gigantocellular tegmental field (FTG) (p. 495)

LEARNING OBJECTIVES FOR CHAPTER 15

When you have mastered the material in the chapter, you will be able to:

LESSON 1: BIOLOGICAL CLOCKS, THE SUPRACHIASMATIC NUCLEUS AND
BRAINSTEM INVOLVEMENT IN THE SLEEP-WAKING CYCLE

1. Describe the evidence for the existence of biological clocks and Zeitgebers.

2. Describe the anatomy of the suprachiasmatic nucleus of the hypothalamus and its function in circadian rhythms in mammals.

3. Summarize the conclusions drawn about brainstem mechanisms of the sleep-waking cycle based on the cerveau isolé, encéphale isolé and midpontine pretrigeminal transections.

4. Summarize the evidence that the reticular formation of the brainstem has a crucial role in arousal.

5. Describe the roles of the dopaminergic and noradrenergic systems in arousal.

6. Describe the role of the raphe (and serotonin) and the nucleus of the solitary tract in brainstem sleep mechanisms.

7. Explain the role of the pontine reticular formation and neurotransmitter systems of the pons in D sleep.

8. Evaluate the hypothesis that the gigantocellular tegmental field is involved in the initiation of D sleep.

9. Summarize the evidence for the existence of forebrain waking and sleeping mechanisms.

LESSON 1: BIOLOGICAL CLOCKS, THE SUPRACHIASMATIC NUCLEUS AND
BRAINSTEM INVOLVEMENT IN THE SLEEP-WAKING CYCLE


```
OBJECTIVE 15-1:  Describe the evidence for the existence of biological
                 clocks and Zeitgebers.
```

1. How are the concepts of biological clocks, circadian rhythms and Zeitgebers related? (pp. 471-474)

2. Explain why we believe that the sleep-waking cycle and circadian temperature rhythms are controlled by different biological clocks. (p. 474)


```
OBJECTIVE 15-2:  Describe the anatomy of the suprachiasmatic nucleus
                 of the hypothalamus and its function in circadian
                 rhythms in mammals.
```

3. Describe the special anatomical characteristics of the suprachiasmatic nucleus (SCN) of the medial hypothalamus. (p. 474)

4. Draw a schematic diagram showing the afferent inputs and efferent outputs of the SCN. (pp. 474-475)

5. Why do we conclude that not all the behavioral and hormonal functions of the SCN are controlled by the same set of efferent projection fibers? (p. 475)

6. Explain the logic and conclusions of Schwartz and Gainer's (1977) radioactive 2-DG study of the SCN. (pp. 475-476)

7. Some researchers have suggested that protein synthesis within some set of neurons serves as a biological time base. What evidence supports this hypothesis? (pp. 476-477)

OBJECTIVE 15-3: Summarize the conclusions drawn about brainstem mechanisms of the sleep-waking cycle based on the cerveau isolé, encéphale isolé and midpontine pretrigeminal transections.

8. What evidence supports the hypothesis that sleep is an active brain process? (p. 479)

9. Below is a saggittal view of the cat brain. Indicate which transection represents the cerveau isolé and encéphale isolé preparations. What are the effects of each transection on the sleep-waking cycle? (pp. 479-480)

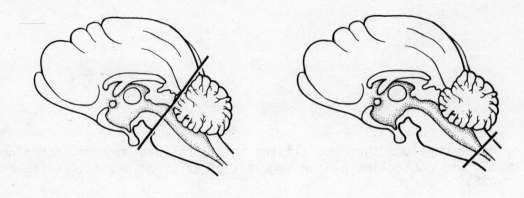

10. What did Bremer (1937) conclude about the causes of sleep on the basis of the above experiments? (p. 481)

11. Describe the experiments of the late 1950's that showed Bremer's conclusions to be incorrect. (p. 481)

12. The diagram below is a schematic summary of the three brainstem tran-
    sections described previously. Label each transection and indicate the
    effects of each on the sleep-waking behavior of cats. What conclusions
    can be drawn about brainstem mechanisms of sleep and arousal from these
    experiments? (pp. 481-482)

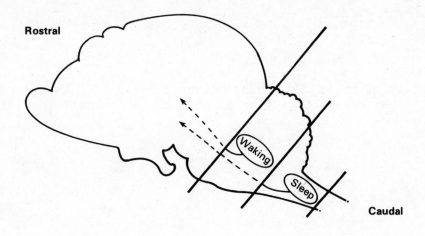

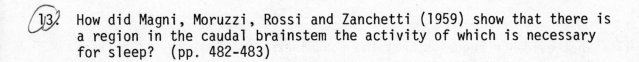

OBJECTIVE 15-4: Summarize the evidence that the reticular formation
                of the brainstem has a crucial role in arousal.

13. How did Magni, Moruzzi, Rossi and Zanchetti (1959) show that there is
    a region in the caudal brainstem the activity of which is necessary
    for sleep? (pp. 482-483)

14. Give evidence from electrical stimulation and lesion studies that the reticular formation is involved in arousal. (p. 483)

15. What was Lindsley et al.'s (1950) explanation for the effects of medial and lateral lesions of the brainstem on arousal in the cat? (pp. 483-484)

LESSON 2: NEUROCHEMICAL AND ELECTROPHYSIOLOGICAL
MECHANISMS OF SLEEP AND AROUSAL

OBJECTIVE 15-5: Describe the roles of the dopaminergic and noradrenergic systems in arousal.

16. Two brainstem arousal mechanisms have been hypothesized, the dopamine and norepinephrine systems. Where are the cell bodies of the proposed dopamine system located? (pp. 484-485)

_____

17. What evidence suggests that the dopaminergic system may not be necessary for behavioral arousal? (pp. 484-485)

18. What evidence suggests, however, that the dopamine system does play a role in mediating arousal? (p. 485)

19. From what structure does the noradrenergic system arise? (p. 485)

the rostral portion of the locus coeruleus
(a structure in the dorsal pons

20. What are the effects of lesioning the dorsal noradrenergic pathway? (p. 485)

hypersomnia

What are the effects of electrically stimulating the dorsal noradrenergic pathway? (p. 486)

arousal

Conclusions?

OBJECTIVE 15-6: Describe the role of the raphe (and serotonin) and the nucleus of the solitary tract in brainstem sleep mechanisms.

---

21. Label the figure below, indicating the position of the raphe nucleus relative to other brainstem structures. (p. 487)

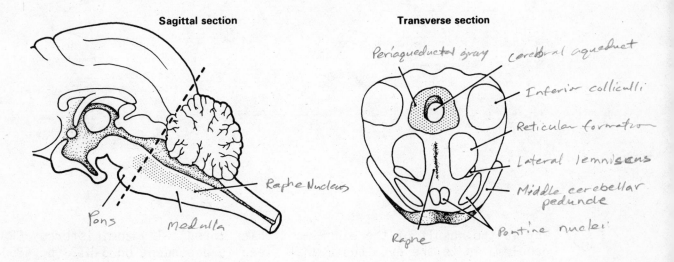

Sagittal section

Raphe Nucleus

Pons

Medulla

Transverse section

Periaqueductal gray

cerebral aqueduct

Inferior colliculli

Reticular formation

Lateral lemniscus

Middle cerebellar peduncle

Pontine nuclei

Raphe

22. What are the effects of raphe lesions on the sleep-waking cycle?
(p. 487)

23. What neurotransmitter is located in the raphe? (p. 487)_____

How can brain 5-HT be depleted by means other than raphe lesions?
(p. 487)

24. Below are graphs from two experiments that have related serotonin to
sleep mechanisms. Using these graphs, explain the effects of (a) a
single injection of para-chlorophenylalanine and (b) chronic administration of PCPA on sleep. (pp. 488-489)

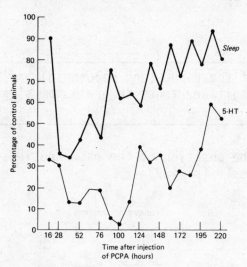 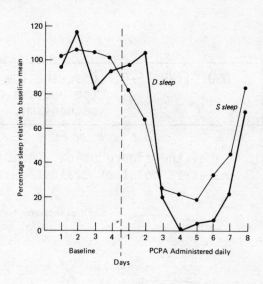

25. Why is the result of the experiment which chronically administered PCPA
problematic to the hypothesis that sleep is dependent on 5-HT? (p. 489)

26. What are the effects of chronic PCPA administration on the phasic aspects of D sleep? (p. 489)

27. What are the effects of cooling the medulla? Explain. (p. 490)

28. How is the nucleus of the solitary tract related to the previous experiment? (p. 490)

29. What kind of afferent information does this nucleus receive? (p. 490)

30. What are the effects of stimulation of the nucleus of the solitary tract on the EEG? (p. 490)

How might the nucleus of the solitary tract be involved in the sleepiness induced by gentle rocking or a large meal? (p. 491)

31. Describe the functional relations between the midbrain reticular system and the nucleus of the solitary tract. (p. 491)

OBJECTIVE 15-7: Explain the role of the pontine reticular formation and neurotransmitter systems of the pons in D sleep.

---

32. Explain why Jouvet's (1962) transection and lesion experiments suggest that an important D sleep mechanism lies within the pons. (pp. 491-492)

33. What evidence has led to the conclusion that descending efferents of the locus coeruleus are important in mediating the muscular inhibition during D sleep, but do not appear to be involved in the initiation of D sleep? (pp. 492-493)

34. There is a great deal of pharmacological evidence that norepinephrine and dopamine are important in D sleep. Next to each drug listed below, indicate the neurochemical action and its effects on D sleep. (p. 493)

Drug	Mechanism of Action	Effect on D Sleep
alpha-methyl paratyrosine		
reserpine		
propranolol		
pimozide		
amphetamine		
tricyclic antidepressants		

What can be concluded from all these data?

35. What is the link between depression and D sleep? (pp. 493-494)

36. There is pharmacological evidence from humans that suggests that serotonergic neurons exert an inhibitory effect on brain mechamisms that are active during D sleep. Next to each serotonergic drug below, indicate its mechanism of action and its effect on D sleep. (p. 494)

Drug	Mechanism of Action	Effect on D Sleep
PCPA		
LSD/mescaline		
MAO inhibitors		
imipramine		

What can be concluded from all these experiments?

255

37. Acetylcholine has also been linked to D sleep. Indicate the mechanism and effects of the cholinergic drugs below. (pp. 494-495)

Drug	Mechanism of Action	Effect on D Sleep
organophosphate insecticides		
physostigmine		

38. The drug experiments above suggest that cholinergic neurons are involved in D sleep. What pharmacological evidence demonstrates that the important cholinergic mechanisms reside in the pons? (pp. 494-495)

39. Describe the experiment which showed that hypersensitive cholinergic mechanisms might be an underlying factor that predisposes certain individuals to bouts of clinical depression. (p. 495)

```
OBJECTIVE 15-8:   Evaluate the hypothesis that the gigantocellular
                  tegmental field is involved in the initiation of
                  D sleep.
```

40. What is it about the anatomy and axonal projections of the gigantocellular tegmental field (FTG) that makes it a likely candidate for the control of the sleep-waking cycle? (p. 495)

41. Describe the electrophysiological study that first implicated the FTG in the initiation of D sleep. (p. 495)

42. What recent evidence argues that the FTG is <u>not</u> an initiator of D sleep, but rather the FTG is associated with motor mechanisms? (pp. 496-497)

43. Now, try to integrate all the information you learned from Pages 491-497. Next to each neurotransmitter or anatomical structure, indicate the conclusions we can draw at this point regarding the neural bases of D sleep.

a. serotonergic neurons of the dorsal raphe

b. descending noradrenergic efferents of the locus coeruleus

c. ascending noradrenergic efferents of the locus coeruleus

d. cholinergic neurons in the central pons

e. gigantocellular tegmental field

OBJECTIVE 15-9: Summarize the evidence for the existence of forebrain waking and sleeping mechanisms.

---

44. What evidence suggests that there exists a forebrain arousal mechanism? (p. 498)

45. Why is it premature to conclude that the posterior hypothalamus is a forebrain "waking center"? (pp. 498-499)

46. List the experimental evidence that suggests that the basal forebrain contains sleep-promoting mechanisms. (pp. 499-501)

47. Describe the reciprocal interaction of the preoptic area with the reticular formation. (p. 501)

48. Summarize the evidence that supports the hypothesis that the preoptic area is an important forebrain waking structure. (p. 501)

Integrative and Thought Questions

1. In Chapter 14, you learned about several sleep disorders, including narcolepsy, cataplexy, insomnia, hypnogogic hallucinations and somnambulism. Given what you now know about the physiology and neurochemistry of the sleep-waking cycle, try to generate plausible explanations for these "disorders".

2. Relate the information in this chapter concerning the physiology and neurochemistry of sleep to the two general theories of why we sleep discussed in the last chapter.

3. Many people claim to have "mental alarm clocks", i.e., the ability to wake up precisely at a prespecified time. How might it be possible for a brain, cycling between S and D sleep, to "know" how much real clock time has elapsed and to produce cortical desynchrony and arousal at the appropriate waking time?

16

Emotion, Aggression, and Species-Typical Behavior

Essential Concepts

1. According to the James-Lange theory, the experience of emotions is the result of feedback from the peripheral effects of the autonomic nervous system and from skeletal muscles. While this theory has been criticized, self-report data from humans with severed spinal cords suggest that the feelings or experience of emotions depends somewhat on feedback from the body to the brain.

2. It has been possible to study the neural bases of some of the many types of aggression since electrical stimulation of the brain can elicit at least three types of aggressive behavior: irritable aggression (affective attack), predatory attack (quiet-biting attack) and fear-induced aggression.

3. Quiet-biting attack and affective attack are both behaviorally and physiologically distinct, but neither seems to be related to the neural circuits involved in hunger. ESB that produces affective attack has been shown to be aversive, while that eliciting quiet-biting attack is generally reinforcing. Amphetamines accentuate affective attack but diminish quiet-biting attack. Affective attack may be produced by medial hypothalamic stimulation, whereas quiet-biting attack is elicited by lateral hypothalamic stimulation. Both kinds of aggression appear to be mediated by the periaqueductal gray of the midbrain. Electrical stimulation of the hypothalamus or periaqueductal gray facilitates the sensory and motor mechanisms involved in attack. Two limbic system structures, the amygdala and the septum, have a modulatory role in emotional behavior.

4. Inter-male aggression is suppressed by adrenocorticotrophic hormone (ACTH) and this suppression is independent of the inhibitory effects of ACTH on testosterone secretion. However, testosterone is necessary for inter-male aggression.

5. Severe emotional disturbances in humans have, on occasion, been treated by psychosurgery, the rationale for which is usually based on lesion

experiments with animals. Amygdala lesions have been performed in an attempt to control violent behavior. The VMH of persons with serious sexual behavior disorders has been ablated. Two major criticisms may be leveled at present-day psychosurgery. First, although psychosurgery may ameliorate some instances of violence, clinical evaluations of these procedures have been inadequate to provide conclusive evidence. Second, animal research has not yet provided us with a clear understanding of the neural mechanisms underlying aggression to justify brain ablation in humans.

6. Maternal behavior of many nonhuman species consists of a complex set of species-typical behaviors: nest-building, cleaning, nursing and retrieving young. Nest-building behavior is dependent upon progesterone in pregnant mice, while prolactin facilitates nest-building following parturition. Prolactin also plays an important role in the initiation of maternal behavior.

7. The most critical region involved in maternal behavior is the medial preoptic area of the hypothalamus. Various lesions of the limbic system, the cingulate cortex and the septum, impair maternal behavior. Lesions of the cingulate cortex disrupt the sequence but not the elements of maternal behavior, while destruction of the septum severely impairs any species-typical patterns requiring spatial orientation.

Key Words

James-Lange theory (p. 504)

affective attack (p. 509)

quiet-biting attack (p. 509)

species-typical behavior (p. 510)

periaqueductal gray (p. 512)

corticomedial nuclei of the amygdala (p. 514)

basolateral nuclei of the amygdala (p. 514)

stria terminalis (p. 514)

ventral amygdalofugal pathway (p. 514)

adrenocorticotrophic hormone (ACTH) (p. 518)

psychosurgery (p. 520)

superfetation (p. 528)

gestation (p. 528)

parturition (p. 528)

concaveation (p. 530)

progesterone (p. 531)

prolactin (p. 532)

medial preoptic area (p. 533)

cingulate cortex (p. 534)

septum (p. 534)

LEARNING OBJECTIVES FOR CHAPTER 16

When you have mastered the material in the chapter, you will
be able to:

1. Describe the James-Lange theory of emotions and discuss the evidence for
   and against this explanation for emotion.

2. Give examples of the various types of aggression and the importance of
   this classification scheme to our understanding of the neural bases of
   aggression.

3. Describe the neural and sensory systems involved in aggressive attack
   which is elicited by electrical stimulation of the brain.

4. Describe the anatomical pathways of the limbic system and the role of
   the limbic system in mediating and modulating emotional behavior.

5. Identify and describe the hormonal influences on aggression.

6. Evaluate the use and outcome of psychosurgery in the "treatment" of
   human violence.

7. Describe maternal behavior in nonhuman animals.

8. Describe what we know about the hormonal and neural mechanisms of maternal behavior.

OBJECTIVE 16-1: Describe the James-Lange theory of emotions and
discuss the evidence for and against this explanation for emotion.

---

1. What are some of the difficulties that the study of emotions presents to the experimental psychologist? (p. 504)

2. Outline the James-Lange theory of emotions and give an original example of how the theory explains some particular emotional experience. (pp. 504-505).

3. What was William Cannon's critique of the James-Lange theory? (p. 505)

4. Explain how Hohman's (1966) study of people with severed spinal cords and Sweet's (1966) report of a person with unilateral damage to the sympathetic ANS support the James-Lange theory. (pp. 505-507)

(5) List and give original examples of the seven classes of aggression identified by Moyer (1976). (p. 508)

6. Behaviorally distinguish between the two major types of aggression elicited by brain stimulation. (p. 509)

(7) What kinds of evidence allow us to conclude that certain types of aggressive behavior are "species-typical" and unlearned? (p. 510)

8. Explain how we know that neither quiet-biting attack nor predatory attack
are mediated by or related to the neural mechanisms involved in hunger.
(pp. 510-511)

9. How do we know that electrical brain stimulation that induces affective attack is aversive? (p. 511)

OBJECTIVE 16-3: Describe the neural and sensory systems involved in aggressive attack which is elicited by electrical stimulation of the brain.

---

10. Indicate which, if any, species-typical behavior patterns result from electrical stimulation in each of the hypothalamic areas listed below. (p. 511)

a. medial hypothalamus _____

b. lateral hypothalamus _____

c. dorsal hypothalamus _____

11. Describe the experimental evidence that indicates that the effects of hypothalamic brain stimulation are mediated caudally through the midbrain. (pp. 511-512)

12. Explain the logic and results of Ellison and Flynn's (1968) hypothalamic island experiment. (p. 512)

13. Below are three major conclusions based on Flynn and his colleagues' work concerning the neural and sensory mechanisms of aggression elicited by brain stimulation. Give the experimental evidence that led to each conclusion. (pp. 513-514)

a. Stimulation of the midbrain that produces aggression does so via motor mechanisms and not by producing some emotional antecedents of the attack.

b. Stimulation of the hypothalamus or midbrain facilitates the sensory and motor mechanisms involved in attack and defensive behavior.

c. The periaqueductal gray is critical for the organization of the behavior patterns involved in attack.

OBJECTIVE 16-4: Describe the anatomical pathways of the limbic system and the role of the limbic system in mediating and modulating emotional behavior.

---

14. On the following page, draw a diagram showing the pathways interconnecting the amygdala, olfactory bulb, septum and hypothalamus. Label the major fiber tracts. (pp. 514-515)

15. Name the two principal subdivisions of the amygdaloid complex and describe the neural pathways by which each region connects with the
hypothalamus. (p. 514)

16. Cite the evidence showing that the subdivisions of the amygdala modu-
late aggression. (p. 515)

17. The amygdala's role in aggression seems to be intimately involved with
the hypothalamus. Cite evidence for this statement. (p. 516)

18. Which amygdaloid-hypothalamic pathway seems to be most involved in aggression? (p. 516)_____

Explain.

19. What experimental evidence allows us to draw the conclusion that the septum is involved in inhibiting attack and flight? (p. 516)

20. Why does the "septal rage syndrome" in rodents support the notion that the septum has an inhibitory role in emotional behavior? (p. 516)

OBJECTIVE 16-5: Identify and describe the hormonal influences on aggression.

21. Give three pieces of evidence in humans and other animals that androgen-sensitive neural circuits underly some kinds of aggression. (p. 517)

22. Why are the hormones released by the adrenal glands believed to be important in inter-male aggression? (p. 518)

23. Explain how Leshner and his co-workers (1973) set about to determine which hormone(s) were responsible for the decreased inter-male aggression observed after adrenalectomy. (p. 519)

What were the conclusions drawn from these experiments regarding the role of ACTH and testosterone in inter-male aggression? (p. 519)

OBJECTIVE 16-6: Evaluate the use and outcome of psychosurgery in the "treatment" of human violence.

 24. Is there a causal relation between overcrowding and human violence? Explain. (p. 519)

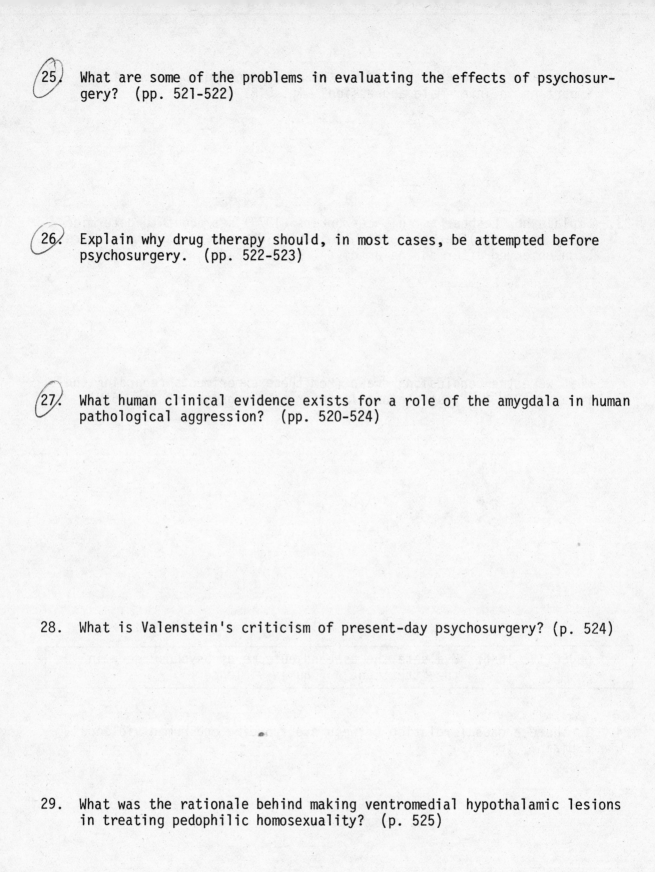

25. What are some of the problems in evaluating the effects of psychosurgery? (pp. 521-522)

26. Explain why drug therapy should, in most cases, be attempted before psychosurgery. (pp. 522-523)

27. What human clinical evidence exists for a role of the amygdala in human pathological aggression? (pp. 520-524)

28. What is Valenstein's criticism of present-day psychosurgery? (p. 524)

29. What was the rationale behind making ventromedial hypothalamic lesions in treating pedophilic homosexuality? (p. 525)

What is the problem with this reasoning?

30. What is the rationale for performing amygdalectomies in the treatment of extreme human violence? (p. 525)

31. Sometimes experimental data from lesion experiments with animals are generalized to human cases by neurosurgeons. Amygdalectomy seems to have more than simply a "taming" effect on monkeys. What are some of these effects? (pp. 525-526)

32. Give a general critique of psychosurgery as a means to control human violence. (pp. 520-526)

OBJECTIVE 16-7: Describe maternal behavior in nonhuman animals.

---

33. What might be the biological adaptive significance of the fact that mammalian young are born in an immature state? (pp. 527-528)

34. What maternal behaviors occur during (a) gestation and (b) parturition? (pp. 528-529)

35. What is the adaptive importance, for both rodent mothers and pups, of anogenital licking? (p. 529)

36. What stimuli are important in eliciting the various aspects of maternal behavior in both virgin and experienced female rodents? (pp. 530-531)

37. What other functions do the olfactory bulbs have in maternal behavior besides simply transmitting olfactory information to the brain? (p. 531)

OBJECTIVE 16-8: Describe what we know about the hormonal and neural mechanisms of maternal behavior.

---

38. Which two hormones facilitate nest-building in female rodents? When are each of these hormones most effective? (pp. 531-532)

39. Explain how we know that the experience of parturition is not necessary for the initiation of maternal behavior. (p. 533)

40. What experimental evidence suggests that prolactin may not be the only hormonal factor involved in the initiation of maternal behavior? (p. 533)

41. What area of the brain seems to be most critical in mediating maternal behavior? Cite the evidence. (p. 533)

42. The limbic system has also been shown to be involved in maternal behavior. Indicate the effects on maternal behavior of destruction of the limbic structures below. (p. 534)

a) cingulate cortex

b) septum

43. While destruction of the septum severely impairs nearly all aspects of maternal behavior, more recent evidence suggests that septal lesions impair only those species-typical behaviors that require spatial orientation. Explain. (p. 534)

44. On what experimental findings is the above conclusion based? (p. 534)

Thought Question

1. Do you think there is any way for the physiological psychologist to study
    the physiological bases of feelings and the experience of emotions inde-
    pendent and apart from overt emotional behavior?

17

Reward and Punishment

Essential Concepts

1. The principle of natural selection and the principle of reinforcement
    are useful in explaining the adaptibility of species and individual
    organisms over time. The behavior of higher organisms is changed by its
    consequences. Positively reinforcing stimuli increase the probability
    of the behavior that immediately preceded it. Punishing stimuli
    decrease the probability of the response that immediately preceded it.
    Our understanding of the physiological mechanisms responsible for
    operant conditioning began with the discovery that electrical stimulation
    (ESB) of the medial forebrain bundle can serve as a positive reinforcer
    for a response such as lever pressing.

2. The reinforcing effects of ESB do not seem to be due to drive reduction.
    Rather, reinforcing ESB appears to increase nonspecific arousal or drive.
    The reinforcing effects of ESB are increased when the level of natural
    drive is increased. ESB also elicits specific behaviors like eating and
    drinking. The presence of appetitive stimuli can increase the reinforc-
    ing effect of ESB. Positive feedback theories of ESB propose that the
    drive-increasing effect of ESB is reinforcing. These theories are
    supported by the fact that responding for ESB usually decreases when
    there is no opportunity to respond for several hours (overnight decrement
    and priming effect) and the fact that responding for ESB rapidly
    extinguishes following the withdrawal of brain stimulation.

3. Neuroanatomical and pharmacological studies have shown that the
    catecholamine pathways mediate the reinforcing effects of ESB.
    The mesolimbic dopaminergic system seems to be especially important in
    the reinforcing effect of ESB.

4. Some fear that ESB could be used to control human behavior. However, two
    arguments speak against this fear. First, if a population of people were
    sufficiently controlled to permit electrode implantation then tyrannical
    control is already in effect. Second, ESB has not yet been found to

be very effective in humans.

5. Pain messages arise from two types of peripheral pain fibers (C and A-delta fibers) which synapse in the dorsal horn of the spinal cord and ascend via the spinothalamic and spinoreticulothalamic tracts to the thalamus. Pain messages from the head and face travel to the CNS via the trigeminothalamic and trigeminoreticulothalamic tracts.

6. Neurosurgical treatments for intractable pain have shown that the perception and emotional effects (or tolerance) of pain involve separate mechanisms. Opiate drugs produce analgesia by stimulating neurons in the periaqueductal gray. These neurons send axons to the nucleus raphe magnus in the medulla which in turn projects neurons down into the spinal cord via the dorsolateral columns.

7. The brain contains endogenous opiate receptors and produces its own opiate-like substances, enkephalins and endorphins. The release of endogenous opiates may underlie the effects of acupuncture and placebos as well as mediate the effects of learned helplessness. Endorphins also act as neurotransmitters in interneurons within the dorsal horn. These interneurons may be involved in spinal mechanisms of natural analgesia. There is also some evidence that endorphins are involved in reinforcement mechanisms.

Key Terms

reinforcement (p. 537)

punishment (p. 537)

need reduction hypothesis (p. 538)

drive reduction hypothesis (p. 538)

medial forebrain bundle (p. 542)

appetitive stimulus (p. 545)

priming (p. 546)

central tegmental tract (p. 556)

dorsal tegmental tract (p. 556)

subcoeruleus cell group (p. 556)

locus coeruleus (p. 556)

nigrostriatal system (p. 556)

mesolimbic dopamine system (p. 556)

pars compacta (p. 556)

neostriatum (p. 556)

ventral tegmental area (VTA) (p. 557)

sulcal cortex (p. 561)

C fiber (p. 570)

A-delta fiber (p. 570)

spinothalamic tract (p. 570)

spinoreticulothalamic tract (p. 570)

trigeminoreticulothalamic tract (p. 570)

anterior trigeminothalamic tract (p. 570)

prefrontal lobotomy (p. 571)

prefrontal leucotomy (p. 571)

analgesia (p. 571)

endogenous opiate (p. 571)

endorphin (p. 571)

naloxone (p. 572)

dihydromorphine (p. 572)

nucleus raphe magnus (p. 572)

dorsolateral column (p. 572)

enkephalin (p. 573)

β-endorphin (p. 574)

placebo (p. 574)

LEARNING OBJECTIVES FOR CHAPTER 17

When you have mastered the material in this chapter you will
be able to:

LESSON 1 POSITIVE REINFORCEMENT AND REINFORCING BRAIN STIMULATION

1. Describe the behavioral processes of reinforcement and punishment, then
explain the relation of these learning processes to the concepts of
natural selection and drive.

2. Discuss the discovery and the significance of reinforcing brain
stimulation.

3. Describe the neuroanatomical and neurochemical substrates of reinforcing
brain stimulation.

4. Discuss the possibility that ESB could be used in the control of human
behavior.

LESSON 2 THE NEURAL AND NEUROCHEMICAL MECHANISMS OF PAIN

5. Describe the neural mechanisms responsible for the perception and
emotional effects of painful stimuli.

6. Explain how opiate drugs, such as morphine, work to alleviate pain.

7. Discuss the biological significance of endogenous opiates.

LESSON 1 POSITIVE REINFORCEMENT AND REINFORCING BRAIN STIMULATION

> OBJECTIVE 17-1: Describe the behavioral processes of reinforcement and
> punishment, then explain the relation of these learning
> processes to the concepts of natural selection and
> drive.

1. In what ways are the principle of natural selection and the principle of
reinforcement similar? (pp. 536-537)

2. Define and give original examples of reinforcement and punishment. (p. 537)

3. What is the major difficulty with the need reduction hypothesis of reinforcement? (p. 538)

4. What criticisms have been made of the drive reduction hypothesis. (pp. 538-539)

OBJECTIVE 17-2: Discuss the discovery and significance of reinforcing brain stimulation.

---

5. Explain the serendipitous way in which Olds and Milner (1954) discovered the reinforcing effects of brain stimulation. (pp. 540-541)

6. Give evidence that the reinforcing effect of electrical stimulation of the brain (ESB) is very potent. (pp. 541-542)

7. On what bases can it be said that the immediate effect of most natural reinforcers is not to reduce drive, but to increase it? (p. 543)

8. What evidence allows us to conclude that ESB is more reinforcing when an animal's drive state is increased?(p. 544)

9. What is the effect of the presence of an appetitive stimulus during ESB? (p. 545)

10. Explain how Maxim (1972, 1977) showed that aversive stimuli can also increase responding for ESB. (p. 546)

11. What appears to be the best explanation for the "overnight decrement" and "priming effect" of ESB? (pp. 546-547)

12. Give an example of the concept of nonspecific arousal. (pp. 548-549)

13. Why do the effects induced by the tail pinch procedure give credence to the nonspecific arousal hypothesis? (pp. 548-549)

14. Evaluate the hypothesis that ESB produces nonspecific arousal. (p. 550)

15. What is a plausible explanation for the fact that ESB can have both reinforcing and aversive effects? (pp. 550-551)

16. How did Olds and his co-workers (1971) try to demonstrate that hunger and thirst mechanisms can be separated from reinforcement mechanisms? (p. 552)

17. In what way is the reinforcing effect of ESB similar to the reinforcing effect of highly palatable foods in sated animals? (pp. 552-553)

18. Explain how Mendelson's (1966) experiment helps to answer the question of whether drive reduction is a sufficient condition for reinforcement. (p. 554)

OBJECTIVE 17-3: Describe the neuroanatomical and neurochemical substrates of reinforcing brain stimulation.

---

19. Give two pieces of evidence that link the catecholamine systems of the brain to the reinforcing effects of electrical brain stimulation. (pp. 555-556)

20. In the space below, draw the anatomical pathways of the noradrenergic and dopaminergic systems. (p. 557)

21. How did the experiments of Clavier, Fibiger and Phillips (1976) and Cooper, Konkol and Breese (1978) demonstrate that the ascending noradrenergic efferents of the locus coeruleus are not necessary for the reinforcing effects of ESB? (p. 558-559)

22. Below is a list of drugs with either agonist or antagonist effects on catecholamine neurons. Indicate the mechanism of action and the effects of each drug on the reinforcing effects of ESB. (pp. 559-560)

DRUG	MECHANISM OF ACTION	EFFECT
amphetamine		
cocaine		
α-methyl-paratyrosine		
chlorpromazine		
reserpine		
disulfuram		
FLA 63		

Conclusions?

23.   List the evidence which indicates that the dopamine systems are
      important in mediating the reinforcing effects of ESB. (p. 560)

24.   Name the areas of the brain which contain the cell bodies of the
      principle dopaminergic pathways. (p. 560)

      _____   _____

25.   What evidence suggests that the mesolimbic dopaminergic pathway plays an
      especially important role in reinforcement mechanisms? (pp. 560-561)

26.   What is the effect of administering a variety of dopaminergic receptor
      blocking agents on responding for ESB? (p. 564)

27.   How did Fouriezos and Wise (1976) set about to answer the question of
      whether dopamine receptor blockers suppress responding for ESB by
      interfering with reinforcement mechanisms? What conclusions were drawn?
      (p. 564)

28.   Explain the logic of Stein and Ray's (1960) experimental approach to
      the question of why amphetamine increases responding for ESB? What
      was their answer? (pp. 564-565)

29. List the evidence that allows us to conclude that _____ is probably more important in reinforcement mechanisms than NE. (pp. 555-566)

OBJECTIVE 17-4: Discuss the possibility that ESB could be used in the control of human behavior.

30. Some people fear that ESB could become an effective means for controlling human behavior. Outline the two major arguments against this fear. (pp. 566-568)

> OBJECTIVE 17-5: Describe the neural mechanisms responsible for the perception and emotional effects of painful stimuli.

31. What is the adaptive function of pain perception? (p. 568)

32. Describe the morphology and location of pain receptors. (p. 569)

33. Explain how pain information is relayed to the brain from parts of the body below the head. (p. 570)

34. Explain how pain information from the face and head is relayed to the brain. (p. 570)

35. Indicate the effects of lesions in the structures below on the perception and/or tolerance of pain. (pp. 570-571)

ventral nuclei of the thalamus

intralaminar nucleus

parafascicular nucleus

dorsomedial and anterior nuclei

prefrontal cortex

36. Explain why the neurosurgical data in the last question allow us to conclude that pain perception and pain tolerance are independent phenomenon. (pp. 570-571)

37. What evidence suggests that the temporal and/or spatial patterning of incoming pain information is crucial in the CNS coding of somatosensory stimuli? (p. 571)

38. Explain why we can conclude that "sharp" and "dull" pain are mediated by separate systems. (p. 571)

OBJECTIVE 17-6: Explain how opiate drugs, such as morphine, work to alleviate pain.

39. Explain how morphine produces analgesia. (pp. 571-572)

40. How did Pert, Snowman and Snyder (1974) demonstrate the existence of opiate receptors in the brain? (p. 572)

41. Below is a diagram showing the neural mechanisms responsible for the analgesia produced by opiates. Explain, step by step, how opiates work. (pp. 572-573)

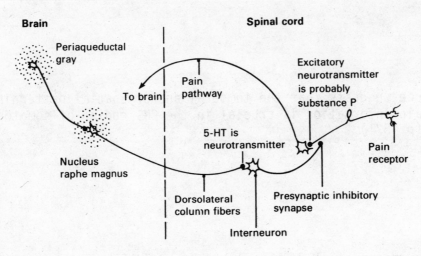

42. Present the experimental evidence for this model by indicating the effects of the following procedures. (pp. 572-573)

microinjection of morphine into the periaqueductal gray

electrical recording of neurons in the periaqueductal gray following systemic injection of morphine

electrical stimulation of the periaqueductal gray

electrical recording of neurons in the raphe following morphine administration lesioning of the nucleus raphe magnus

electrical stimulation of the raphe following lesions of the dorsolateral columns

administration of parachlorophenylalanine

administration of morphine following lesions of the dorsolateral columns

microinjection of serotonin into the spinal cord.

OBJECTIVE 17-7: Discuss the biological significance of endogenous opiates.

---

43. Describe the various types of endogenous opiates and explain how they were discovered. (pp. 573-574)

44. What evidence allows us to conclude that the analgesic effects of acupuncture and placebos are caused by the release of endorphins? (p. 574)

45. Describe the phenomenon of learned helplessness. (p. 575)

46. Describe the experimental evidence which indicates that learned helplessness is mediated by the analgesia produced by endorphin release.
(p. 575)

47. What explanation has been given for the fact that naloxone injections
eliminate an animal's preference for signalled shock? (p. 575)

48. Electrical stimulation of the _____ results in
analgesia equivalent to a dose of 10 mg/kg morphine. (p. 576)

49. Is there any causal link between reinforcing and analgesia-producing
brain stimulation? Explain. (p. 576)

50. Below is a schematic representation of the current hypothesis proposed to explain the fact that naloxone (as well as 5-HT antagonists) block the analgesia that occurs when the nucleus raphe magnus is stimulated. Explain how endorphinergic interneurons may account for these results. (pp. 576-577)

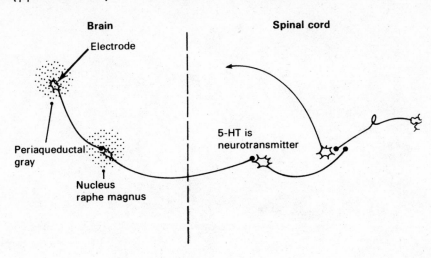

51. What experimental evidence supports the hypothesis that endorphins act as neurotransmitters in the dorsal horn? (p. 577)

52. What evidence suggests that endorphins may be involved in reinforcement mechanisms? (p. 578)

53. What do you suppose is the biological significance of the fact that the brain contains opiate receptors and endogenous opiates? (pp. 575-578)

Thought Questions

1. Do you think it is possible to explain your own actions, thoughts and feelings in terms of the very general principle of natural selection and the principle of reinforcement (and punishment)?

2. Using the concepts and information presented in this chapter, can you generate a plausible hypothesis for human masochism in which one's behavior is reinforced by painful stimuli?

18

Physiology of Learning and Memory

Essential Concepts

1. Memory has been hypothesized to consist of two stages; short- and long-term memory. Blunt head injury and electroconvulsive shock (ECS) seem to disrupt the neuronal reverberatory process involved in short-term memory and consolidation. Both traumatic head injury and ECS produce retrograde amnesia for events that immediately preceded the disruptive event. It has been suggested that ECS and head injury disrupt the memory consolidation process and/or the cataloging of memories into long-term storage. There is good evidence that reverberatory neuronal activity is responsible for short-term memory.

2. Since the physical changes that occur during the transformation of short-term memory to long-term storage must be permanent, it is reasonable to suppose that these changes are structural in nature. Both enzymatic and structural proteins are likely candidates for playing a a direct role in long-term memory.

3. DNA molecules contain the codes specifying the amino acid sequence of proteins. The message contained within a section of DNA is transcribed to RNA in the cell nucleus, and this newly assembled RNA (messenger RNA) travels to ribosomes, where it controls the assemblage of amino acids into a specific sequence to form a protein.

4. The differential repression of genes by the binding of histone proteins to DNA is responsible for cell differentiation. Nonhistone proteins specifically bind to histone proteins and reverse the inhibition of protein synthesis by histones. The ability of nonhistone proteins to induce RNA synthesis is dependent upon their degree of phosphorylation. Since cyclic AMP and cyclic GMP are indirectly responsible for the phosphorylation of nonhistone proteins, it has been suggested that the conversion of ATP to cyclic AMP or GTP to cyclic GMP during neural stimulation causes DNA derepression through the phosphorylation of certain nonhistone proteins.

5. This model, explaining how neural stimulation can lead to changes in protein synthesis, is supported by (a) the fact that nonspecific visual stimulation alters the rate of protein synthesis in the frog, (b) the imprinting experience in newborn chicks increases the rate of protein synthesis as well as RNA polymerase activity, and (c) avoidance training leads to a brief, but dramatic, increase in phosphorylation of nonhistone protein.

6. Results from experiments attempting to determine whether inhibitors of protein synthesis, such as actinomycin-D, puromycin and acetoxycyclohexamide, can block memory consolidation have been inconclusive, owing to the nonspecific nature of these drugs as well as their inability to completely inhibit protein synthesis.

Key Words

short-term memory (p. 582)

long-term memory (p. 582)

retrograde amnesia (p. 584)

anterograde amnesia (p. 584)

electroconvulsive shock (ECS) (p. 587)

temporal gradient (p. 587)

passive avoidance (p. 587)

reverberation (p. 591)

isolated cortical slab (p. 592)

amino acids (p. 596)

carboxyl group (p. 596)

peptide bond (p. 596)

polypeptide (p. 596)

denatured protein (p. 597)

deoxyribonucleic acid (DNA) (p. 598)

adenine (A) (p. 598)

guanine (G) (p. 598)

cytosine (C) (p. 598)

thymine (T) (p. 598)

ribonucleic acid (RNA) (p. 598)

messenger RNA (p. 598)

codon (p. 598)

uracil (U) (p. 598)

transcription (p. 600)

translation (p. 600)

transfer RNA (p. 600)

anticodon loop (p. 600)

amino acid acceptor end (p. 600)

histone protein (p. 602)

nonhistone protein (p. 602)

nucleosome (p. 602)

RNA polymerase (p. 611)

puromycin (p. 614)

cyclohexamide (p. 614)

acetoxycyclohexamide (p. 614)

LEARNING OBJECTIVES FOR CHAPTER 18

When you have mastered the material in the chapter, you will
be able to:

LESSON 1: STAGES OF THE MEMORY PROCESS

1. Describe and give examples of the two stages of memory and describe the
    effects of traumatic head injury on each.

2. Describe the effects of electroconvulsive shock on memory consolidation.

3. Describe and evaluate the reverberatory hypothesis of short-term memory.

4. Summarize the various approaches neuroscientists have used to elucidate
    the physical changes that constitute long-term memory.

LESSON 2: THE BIOCHEMICAL BASES OF LONG-TERM MEMORY

5. Describe the structure, synthesis and function of proteins.

6. Explain how protein synthesis is regulated and how these control mechanisms may be involved in long-term neural changes.

7. Describe the effects of sensory experience on the structure of neurons.

8. Describe the effect of experience on protein and RNA synthesis in the brain.

9. Explain how the phosphorylation of nonhistone proteins may be involved in long-term memory.

10. Evaluate the effects of experimental inhibition of RNA or protein synthesis on long-term memory.

LESSON 1: STAGES OF THE MEMORY PROCESS

OBJECTIVE 18-1: Describe and give examples of the two stages of memory and describe the effects of traumatic head injury on each.

---

1. Give an original example of short- and long-term memory. (p. 582)

2. Give an original example of retrograde and anterograde amnesia. (p. 584)

3. Explain why retrograde and anterograde amnesia resulting from head injury imply the existence of two memory processes. (p. 585)

4. What aspects of post-traumatic amnesia suggest that consolidation is disrupted? (p. 585)

OBJECTIVE 18-2: Describe the effects of electroconvulsive shock on memory consolidation.

---

5. What was the therapeutic rationale for inducing seizures in psychotic patients? (p. 586)

6. How are the effects of electroconvulsive shock (ECS) on memory similar to the effects of blunt head injury? (p. 587)

7. Below is a graph showing the data obtained from Chorover and Schiller's (1965) ECS experiment. Describe their procedure, then explain what the figure implies about the effect of ECS on memory consolidation. (pp. 587-588)

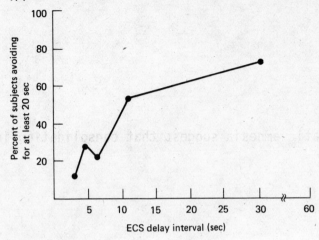

8. How did Robbins and Meyer's (1970) experiment attempt to demonstrate that ECS affects the hypothesized cataloging process? Explain their results. (pp. 589-590)

OBJECTIVE 18-3: Describe and evaluate the reverberatory hypothesis of short-term memory.

---

9. Draw a schematic representation of the concept of a reverberatory circuit. (p. 591)

10. Why has reverberation been hypothesized as the physical basis of short-term memory? (p. 591)

11. Describe Burns' (1958) "isolated cortical slab" experiments that suggested that reverberation does, in fact, occur in the brain. (p. 592)

12. Explain how Verzeano and his co-workers attempted to demonstrate that short-term memories of sensory stimuli are represented by circulating activity between cortex and thalamus. (p. 593)

OBJECTIVE 18-4: Summarize the various approaches neuroscientists
have used to elucidate the physical changes that
constitute long-term memory.

13. Explain why long-term memory is believed to result from stable physical
changes in the brain and not from ongoing neural activity. (pp. 591,593)

14. Summarize the four different approaches neuroscientists have used to
understand the kind of physical changes that constitute long-term memory. What are some of the problems inherent in some of these approaches?
(pp. 594-595)

LESSON 2: THE BIOCHEMICAL BASES OF LONG-TERM MEMORY

OBJECTIVE 18-5: Describe the structure, synthesis and function of
proteins.

15. What are the two general functions of proteins? (p. 595)

16. What are the components of proteins? (p. 596)

_____

17. Diagram the basic structure of amino acids. (p. 596)

18. What is a peptide bond? Diagramatically show how amino acids join together via a peptide bond to form a polypeptide? (pp. 596-597)

19. What is the functional importance of the three-dimensional structure of a protein? (p. 597)

20. Explain how enzyme-substrate binding facilitates chemical reactions. (p. 597)

21. A protein is a string of amino acids. Which cell structure contains the codes for the sequence of amino acids of the proteins that can be produced by a cell? (p. 598)

_____

22. Describe the molecular composition of deoxyribonucleic acid (DNA).
    (p. 598)

23. Draw a schematic diagram showing the structural relationships among the
    four nucleotide bases and the structural backbones of a DNA molecule.
    (p. 598)

24. List the sequence of events involved in protein synthesis. (p. 598)

25. Explain how the four nucleotide bases can specify 64 three-letter codons
    for amino acids. (p. 598)

26. Name the nucleotide sequence codes for "start" and "stop". What is the purpose of these codons? (pp. 598-599)

27. How is RNA produced? How is it different from DNA? (p. 598)

28. Describe the transcriptional process. (pp. 599-600)

29. List all the steps involved in the translational process. (p. 600)

OBJECTIVE 18-6: Explain how protein synthesis is regulated and how these control mechanisms may be involved in long-term neural changes.

30. All cells in an individual organism contain the same DNA molecules. How, then, do we explain the differences in the morphology and function of the various cells that make up a complex organism? (p. 602)

31. What is the function of (a) histone proteins and (b) nonhistone proteins? (p. 602)

32. Describe the mechanism proposed by Stein, Stein and Kleinsmith (1975) to explain how a region of DNA is transformed from an inactive to an active state. (p. 603)

33. List the sequence of steps involving cyclic nucleotides by which neural activity associated with short-term memory leads to changes in protein synthesis necessary for encoding long-term memory. (pp. 603-604)

OBJECTIVE 18-7: Describe the effects of sensory experience on the structure of neurons.

---

34. Growth of new axonal processes might be responsible for long-term neuronal changes. Describe the analogous process in the developing brain. (p. 606)

35. How does Raisman's (1969) experiment show that neurons in the mature CNS are capable of forming new connections? (p. 606)

36. Explain how Spinelli and his co-workers (1979, 1980) demonstrated that learning experiences can change both the structure and function of neurons in somatosensory cortex. (pp. 606-608)

OBJECTIVE 18-8: Describe the effect of experience on protein and RNA synthesis in the brain.

---

37. An experiment conducted by Wegener (1970) demonstrated that neural stimulation increases protein synthesis in localized regions of the frog brain. Explain the rationale, procedure and results of this experiment. (pp. 608-609)

38. Explain why an increase in brain protein synthesis does not necessarily mean that neurons have undergone any physical changes associated with long-term memory. (p. 610)

39. How did Horn, Rose and Bateson (1973) show that sensory stimulation produces changes in RNA and RNA polymerase synthesis? (pp. 610-612)

40. Why would one expect to observe an increase in RNA polymerase activity if RNA synthesis were increased by learning? (pp. 611-612)

```
OBJECTIVE 18-9:   Explain how the phosphorylation of nonhistone
                  proteins may be involved in long-term memory.
```

41. Describe the experimental evidence that demonstrated that avoidance learning increases the phosphorylation of nonhistone proteins. (p. 612)

42. What is the significance of the fact that the change in phosphorylation following avoidance training in rats was brief? (p. 612)

43. Explain why changes in phosphorylation of nonhistone proteins within the nucleus of brain cells is more suggestive of long-term memory storage than within synaptosomes. (pp. 612-613)

44. List the most common protein synthesis inhibitors. (p. 614)

45. Outline the problems inherent in studying long-term memory processes by inhibiting protein or RNA synthesis. (pp. 613-614)

19

Anatomy of Language and Memory

Essential Concepts

1. Karl Lashley first proposed that memories are located diffusely within
   the brain (principle of equipotentiality). However, data from human and
   higher primates indicate that while memories involving a single sense
   modality may be diffusely represented within a particular region of sensory association cortex, complex cross-modal memories, involving information from more than one sensory modality, are mediated by means of specific fiber connections between regions of cortex.

2. In humans, damage to Wernicke's area in the posterior portion of the
   superior temporal gyrus results in a speech comprehension deficit (Wernicke's aphasia) and difficulties in writing of a phonemic language.
   Damage to Broca's area anterior to the face motor area in the frontal
   lobe results in Broca's aphasia, a disorder of speech production. Damage to the arcuate fasciculus, which connects Wernicke's and Broca's
   areas, leads to conduction aphasia, an inability to repeat words and
   phrases. Another clinical example of localized cortical function is
   prosopagnosia, an inability to recognize faces. This disorder results
   from damage to the underside of the temporal and occipital lobes.

3. In nonhuman primates, inferotemporal cortex appears to be involved in
   the storage of complex visual memories. The second somatosensory projection area is necessary for long-term somatosensory memories. A disconnection syndrome can be produced in monkeys by lesioning the periarcuate cortex.

4. Data from brain damaged patients, as well as experiments with nonhuman
   primates, support the conclusion that short-term memories are sensory-
   specific and anatomically distinct. Furthermore, short- and long-term
   memories are located in the same general regions.

5. The human limbic system plays an important role in the consolidation
   process. Patients with Korsakoff's disease have profound anterograde

amnesia. This disorder results from alcoholism-induced damage to the hippocampus or, more reliably, the dorsomedial nucleus of the thalamus. Similar memory impairments are evident in one patient (H.M.) who underwent bilateral medial temporal lobectomy. Until recently, it was believed that the memory deficits were due to damage to the hippocampus. However, damage to the temporal stem, which connects temporal and prefrontal cortex via the dorsomedial nucleus of the thalamus, may be more reliably related to the memory impairments. There is support for the hypothesis that the amnesia of both H.M. and Korsakoff patients involves a deficiency in verbal encoding of information. Amnesic patients show little difficulty in tasks that cannot be mediated verbally. However, when verbal encoding is necessary, severe deficits are observed.

Key Words

engram (p. 617)

equipotentiality (p. 618)

superior temporal gyrus (p. 621)

Wernicke's area (p. 621)

conduction aphasia (p. 626)

arcuate fasciculus (p. 626)

phoneme (p. 629)

phonemic aphasia (p. 630)

dyslexia (p. 631)

planum temporale (p. 632)

prosopagnosia (p. 634)

striate cortex (p. 637)

circumstriate belt (p. 637)

foveal prestriate area (p. 637)

inferotemporal cortex (p. 637)

pulvinar (p. 637)

second somatosensory projection area (SII) (p. 640)

periarcuate cortex (p. 641)

arcuate sulcus (p. 641)

LEARNING OBJECTIVES FOR CHAPTER 19

When you have mastered the material in the chapter, you will
be able to:

LESSON 1: THE ANATOMY OF HUMAN LANGUAGE

1. Evaluate Karl Lashley's principle of equipotentiality of cortical function.

2. Describe the neurolinguistic explanations for Wernicke's and Broca's aphasia.

3. Summarize our current understanding of the causes and characteristics of the following linguistic disorders: conduction aphasia, isolation of the speech areas, phonemic aphasia, dyslexia and prosopagnosia.

LESSON 2: THE ANATOMY OF HUMAN SHORT- AND LONG-TERM MEMORY

4. Discuss the role of inferotemporal cortex, second somatosensory projection area and the periarcuate cortex in memory processes of nonhuman primates.

5. Describe the role of sensory association cortices and their interconnections in short-term memory.

6. Discuss the role of the hippocampus in human memory consolidation.

7. Discuss the role of limbic system circuits in human memory.

LESSON 1: THE ANATOMY OF HUMAN LANGUAGE

OBJECTIVE 19-1: Evaluate Karl Lashley's principle of equipotentiality of cortical function.

---

1. What is the principle of equipotentiality and what evidence supports
this conclusion by Lashley? (pp. 617-618)

2. Describe the experiments which show that learning is possible without
cortex. (pp. 618-619)

OBJECTIVE 19-2: Describe the neurolinguistic explanations of Wernicke's and Broca's aphasia.

---

3. On the following page, draw a diagram of the left hemisphere showing
the location of Wernicke's area, Broca's area and the arcuate fasciculus. (p. 621)

4. Contrast the linguistic impairments that result from damage to either Wernicke's or Broca's area. (pp. 621-622)

5. What is the current explanation of the fact that Wernicke's aphasics often have difficulty in writing? (p. 622)

6. Explain the linguistic impairments resulting from damage to Wernicke's area in the following types of patients. (p. 624)

a. Chinese patients

b. deaf patients

c. Japanese patients

OBJECTIVE 19-3: Summarize our current understanding of the causes and characteristics of the following linguistic disorders: conduction aphasia, isolation of the speech areas, phonemic aphasia, dyslexia and prosopagnosia.

7. What was Norman Geschwind's explanation for conduction aphasia? (p. 626)

8. Explain the severe impairments in the woman whose speech areas were
isolated from the rest of the neocortex as a result of gas poisoning.
(pp. 628-629)

9. Describe the specific linguistic impairments associated with phonemic
aphasia. (pp. 630-631)

10. Explain why neurolinguists believe that dyslexia may be related to
phonemic aphasia. (pp. 631-632)

11. What evidence suggests that dyslexia may result from congenital brain
damage? (pp. 632-633)

12. Describe the behavioral disorder and localized neural damage associated with prosopagnosia. (pp. 634-635)

13. Explain how case studies of localized human brain damage have led to the following three conclusions stated on Page 620. (pp. 620-635)

    a. Both short- and long-term memories are located in the same general regions.

    b. Memories are stored on a sensory-specific basis within cortex.

    c. In humans, specific memories are not limited to particular sense modalities.

OBJECTIVE 19-4: Discuss the role of inferotemporal cortex, second somatosensory projection area and the periarcuate cortex in memory processes of nonhuman primates.

14. Describe the limitations of studying humans in understanding how the brain stores memories and why nonhuman primates have been used in brain research. (pp. 635-636)

15. Diagram the anatomy of the visual system and the connections among striate cortex, circumstriate belt, the inferotemporal cortex and the pulvinar. (pp. 636-638)

16. Describe the "psychic blindness" that results from lesions of temporal cortex in monkeys. (pp. 637-638)

17. Carefully outline the experimental procedure used by Mishkin (1966) which showed that transcortical connections from striate cortex to circumstriate cortex to inferotemporal cortex are involved in visual memory. (p. 638)

18. Summarize the results of Gross' (1973) single unit recording from neurons in inferotemporal cortex of monkeys. What is the significance of these findings? (pp. 638-639)

19. What experimental evidence suggests that the second somatosensory projection area is necessary for long-term somatosensory memories? (p. 640)

20. What is meant by cross-modal learning and memory? (p. 641)

21. Describe the procedure used by Petrides and Iverson (1976) and Cowey and Weiskrantz (1975) to test the formation and retrieval of cross-modal memories in monkeys. (p. 641)

22. What was the result of lesions to periarcuate cortex in monkeys performing cross-modal tasks? Explain the results of this experiment. (p. 641)


```
OBJECTIVE 19-5:  Describe the role of sensory association cortices
                 and their interconnections in short-term memory.
```

23. Give an original, everyday example demonstrating that short-term memories are sensory-specific and anatomically distinct. (pp. 642-643)

24. Describe the memory impairment of the patient, K.F., described by Warrington and Shallice (1972). (pp. 643-644)

25. Using the diagrams below, outline the possible explanations given by Shallice and Warrington (1975) for K.F.'s deficit. (pp. 644-645)

Acoustically-presented material: pathway is indirect

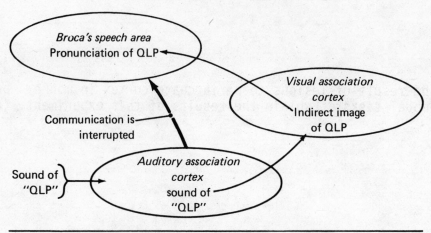

Visually-presented material: pathway is more direct

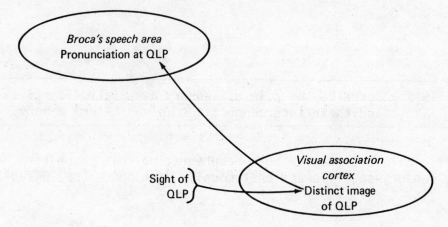

26. Explain why this case study supports the conclusion that visual and auditory short-term memories seem to be located in different parts of the brain. (p. 645)

27. Describe how Kovner and Stamm (1972) showed that inferotemporal cortex is involved in short-term memory in monkeys. (pp. 646-647)

```
┌─────────────────────────────────────────────────────────────────────┐
│  OBJECTIVE 19-6:  Discuss the role of the hippocampus in human memory │
│                   consolidation.                                       │
└─────────────────────────────────────────────────────────────────────┘
```

28. Describe the causes and impairments of Korsakoff's syndrome. (p. 647)

29. Describe the medical and surgical history of Scoville's patient, H.M. (p. 648)

30. Explain why the case of P.B. reported by Penfield and Milner (1958) corroborates the conclusions regarding the causes of anterograde amnesia in H.M. (p. 648)

31. Describe, in detail, H.M.'s memory impairment. (pp. 648-649)

32. Explain why Milner (1970) concluded, on the basis of careful behavioral study of H.M., that the hippocampus plays a vital role in the memory consolidation process. (pp. 649-652)

33. Contrast the memory deficits produced by temporal lobectomy or hippo-
    campal lesions in humans and animals. (p. 652)

34. What explanations have been proposed to account for the discrepancy
    between the effects of hippocampal damage in animals and humans?
    (pp. 652-653)

35. How did Sidman, Stoddard and Mohr (1968) show that H.M.'s ability to
    remember verbal material was superior to his ability to retain non-
    verbal material? (pp. 653-654)

36. Explain how the above experiment and Stewart's (1977) study show that
    H.M.'s amnesia entails a deficit in encoding of information in short-
    term memory. (pp. 655-656)

37. Describe the experimental evidence which suggests that H.M.'s amnesia is the result of deficits in verbal access to stored information. (pp. 656-658)

```
┌─────────────────────────────────────────────────────────────────────┐
│  OBJECTIVE 19-7:  Discuss the role of limbic system circuits in human │
│                   memory.                                             │
└─────────────────────────────────────────────────────────────────────┘
```

38. Draw a schematic diagram of the current concept of Papez's circuit. (pp. 658-659)

39. State Horel's (1978) explanation for the memory impairments produced by temporal lobectomy. (pp. 659-660)

40. Describe the clinical case which supports Horel's hypothesis. (p. 661)

41. Explain why the following hypothesis is plausible: temporal lobectomy results in the kinds of memory impairments seen in H.M. because the connections between anterior temporal cortex and frontal cortex are damaged. (p. 661)

42. Cite the evidence which suggests that while Papez's circuit may not be involved in brain-damage produced amnesia, the dorsomedial nucleus of the thalamus may be the critical structure involved in human memory deficits. (pp. 661-662)

Thought Questions

1. Where would you guess Helen Keller's memories for the spelling of words would be stored?

2. Transcendental and Siddha yoga meditation are said by their practitioners to produce profound relaxation and the experience of "pure consciousness" (as opposed to impure consciousness?). Most meditation techniques involve the silent repetition of a mantra (such as "om nama shivaya"). Can you explain the reported effects of meditation in light of what you have learned about the anatomy of language and memory?

20

Physiology of Mental Disorders

Essential Concepts

1. Two major categories of psychoses have been defined. Schizophrenia is characterized by a disorder of logical thought and the affective psychoses are emotional disorders. There are three types of schizophrenia (paranoid, hebephrenic and catatonic schizophrenia) and two types of affective disorders (bipolar and unipolar affective psychosis). Genetic history is believed to be an important factor in predisposing individuals to develop schizophrenia and affective disorders.

2. The introduction of the first antischizophrenic drug, chlorpromazine, in the 1950s dramatically reduced the number of hospitalized schizophrenic patients. The antischizophrenic action of these drugs appears to be due to their ability to block dopamine receptors in the brain. The potency of a particular drug in inhibiting the binding of ^{3}H-haloperidol has been found to be closely related to its clinical effectiveness. There is evidence that there may be more dopamine receptors in the brains of schizophrenics. The dopamine hypothesis of schizophrenia is supported by the fact that dopamine agonists (such as amphetamine and cocaine) are capable of producing psychotic behavior in normal people and exaccerbates the symptoms of schizophrenic patients.

3. Antischizophrenic drugs require two or three weeks of daily administration before becoming clinically effective. Patients taking these drugs often develop tardive dyskinesia which is worsened by the withdrawal from medication. These two facts have been explained in terms of the development of denervation supersensitivity within dopamine systems.

4. The hypothesis that schizophrenia is a disturbance in selective attention has received support from the fact that unilateral injection of 6-HD into the medial forebrain bundle in rats produces sensory neglect on the contralateral side of the body. Children with hyperkinetic syndrome are often treated with dopamine agoinists such as methylphenidate. Hyperkinesis may be viewed as an attentional deficit while

327

schizophrenia has been hypothesized to be an attentional hypersensitivity.

5. There are three treatments for <u>unipolar depression</u>; ECT, MAO inhibitors, and <u>tricyclic antidepressants</u>. Bipolar disorders are typically treated with <u>lithium carbonate</u>. MAO inhibitors and tricyclic antidepressants are both monoamine agonists. This has led to the suggestion that retarded depression is due to insufficient activity of NE and DA neurons and agitated depression is due to insufficient activity of serotonergic synapses. The fact that <u>reserpine</u> can produce depression in normal people gives support to the view.

6. However, recently-discovered tricyclic drugs, <u>iprindole</u> and <u>mianserin</u>, have little effect on either NE or 5-HT re-uptake. More recent evidence suggests that the common biochemical activity of clinically effective tricyclic antidepressants is their ability to block <u>histamine</u> receptors.

<u>Key Terms</u>

psychoses (p. 664)

schizophrenia (p. 664)

affective disorder (p. 664)

neuroses (p. 664)

paranoid schizophrenia (p. 665)

hebephrenic schizophrenia (p. 665)

catatonic schizophrenia (p. 665)

waxy flexibility (p. 665)

acute schizophrenia (p. 666)

process schizophrenia (p. 666)

chlorpromazine (p. 668)

major tranquilizers (p. 669)

benzodiazepines (p. 670)

flupenthixol (p. 670)

isomer (p. 670)

328

butyrophenone (p. 671)

haloperidol (p. 671)

homovanillic acid (HVA) (p. 675)

dihydroxyphenylacetic acid (DOPAC) (p. 676)

hyperkinetic syndrome (p. 679)

tardive dyskinesia (p. 681)

denervation supersensitivity (p. 681)

affect (p. 682)

bipolar affective disorder (p. 682)

unipolar depression (p. 683)

iproniazid (p. 685)

imipramine (p. 685)

biogenic amine (p. 686)

tricyclic antidepressant (p. 686)

iprindole (p. 687)

mianserin (p. 687)

reserpine (p. 688)

LEARNING OBJECTIVES FOR CHAPTER 20

When you have mastered the material in this chapter, you will be able to:

LESSON 1: SCHIZOPHRENIA

1. Describe the symptoms of schizophrenia and evaluate its heritability.

2. Summarize our current understanding of the neurochemical basis of schizophrenia in light of the pharmacological action of antischizophrenic and dopamine agonist drugs.

3. Describe the biochemical abnormalities of the brains of schizophrenic patients

4. Discuss the attentional hypothesis of schizophrenia and summarize the supporting pharmacological evidence for this view.

LESSON 2: AFFECTIVE PSYCHOSES

5. Describe the symptoms and heritability of both unipolar and bipolar affective disorders.

6. Discuss the four physiological treatments for the affective disorders.

7. Summarize our current understanding of the neurochemical bases of the affective disorders in light of the pharmacological action of the tricyclic antidpressents and MAO inhibitors.

LESSON 1: SCHIZOPHRENIA

OBJECTIVE 20-1: Describe the symptoms of schizophrenia and evaluate its heritability.

---

1. Name the two major categories of psychosis. (p. 664)

_____   _____

2. Differentiate between psychosis and neurosis. (pp. 664-665)

3. What is the origin of the term "schizophrenia" and to what does it refer? (p. 665)

4. Name and characterize the three types of schizophrenia. (p. 665)

5. Differentiate between acute and process schizophrenia. (p. 666)

6. Explain how Kety, Rosenthal, Wender and Schulsinger (1968) demonstrated a relationship between genetics and schizophrenia. (pp. 666-667)

7. What did Heston (1966) discover about the offspring of schizophrenic mothers and why does this add support to Kety et al's contention? (p. 667)

8. Explain why the statistics of schizophrenia argue against the existence of a single "schizophrenia gene". (p. 667)

OBJECTIVE 20-2: Summarize our current understanding of the biochemical basis of schizophrenia in light of the pharmacological action of antischizophrenic and dopamine agonist drugs.

---

9. Describe how antischizophrenic drugs were discovered in the 1940s. (p. 668)

10. Describe the impact of chlorpromazine on the treatment of hospitalized schizophrenic patients in this country using the graph below. (p. 669)

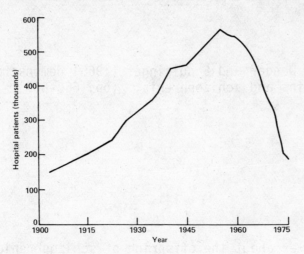

11. What arguments have been made against the popular criticism that antischizophrenic drugs are nothing more than sedatives? (p. 670)

12. Give three pieces of evidence to support the contention that the effective antischizophrenic drugs block postsynaptic dopamine receptors. (pp. 670-671)

13. Explain why Johnstone et al's (1978) study of isomeric forms of flupenthixol supports the dopamine hypothesis of schizophrenia. (pp. 670-671)

14. Describe the effects of antischizophrenic drugs on cyclic AMP as demonstrated by Kebabian, Petzold and Greengard (1972). What is the significance of the experiment? (p. 671)

15. Explain how Snyder, Burt and Creese (1976) demonstrated the existence of two different binding sites on dopamine receptors. (pp. 671-672)

16. What conclusions regarding the mechanism of action of potent antischizophrenic drugs can be drawn from the figure below? (p. 673)

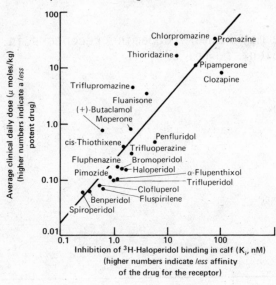

17. Name three dopamine agonists that can produce schizophrenic behavior. Indicate the mechanism of each. What conclusions can be drawn from these effects regarding the neurochemical basis of schizophrenia? (pp. 674-675)

333

18. List some of the possible explanations relating to the suggestion that
    schizophrenia is the result of hyperactivity of dopaminergic synapses.
    (p. 675)

19. What evidence rules against the simplest hypothesis - that more
    dopamine is secreted in the brains of schizophrenics? (p. 675)

20. What study suggested that there may be more dopamine receptors in
    the brains of schizophrenic patients? (p. 676)

21. Describe the attentional hypothesis of schizophrenia. (p. 678)

22. What is the result of unilateral injections of 6-hydroxydopamine into the medial forebrain bundle of rats? Why are the results of this experiment support for the attentional hypothesis? (p. 678-679)

23. Explain why the effective treatment of hyperkinesis in children with catecholamine agonists such as _____ and _____ is relevant to the attentional hypothesis of schizophrenia. (p. 679)

24. How does the time course of the therapeutic effect of antischizophrenic drugs compare to the time course of their effects on dopamine receptors? (p. 680)

25. Why does this differential time course present a problem to the dopamine receptor hypothesis of schizophrenia? (pp. 680-681)

26. Explain how the tardive dyskinesia often produced by antischizophrenic drugs is pharmacologically different from parkinson's disease. (p. 681)

27. How can denervation supersensitivity account for the time course and tardive dyskinesic effects of antischizophrenic drug treatment? (p. 681)

OBJECTIVE 20-5: Describe the symptoms and heritability of both unipolar and bipolar affective disorders.

28. Differentiate between the behavioral characteristics of bipolar and unipolar disorders. (pp. 682-683)

29. What evidence from family histories and concordance rates in MZ twins suggests that genetics plays a role in an individual's susceptibility to affective psychosis? (pp. 684-685)

OBJECTIVE 20-6 : Discuss the four physiological treatments for the affective disorders.

30. Name the four different treatments used with patients suffering from either unipolar or bipolar affective disorders. (p. 685)

31. Contrast the therapeutic time course of the four types of affective disorder treatments. (p. 685)

32. Why is the depression of a bipolar disorder thought to be a reaction to mania, but not the reverse? (pp. 685-686)

OBJECTIVE 20-7: Summarize our current understanding of the neuro-chemical bases of the affective disorders in light of the pharmacological action of the tricyclic anti-depressants and MAO inhibitors.

33. Describe how antidepressant MAO inhibitors were discovered. (p. 686)

34. Describe the mechanism of action of MAO inhibitors. (p. 686)

35. What are the dangerous side-effects of MAO inhibitors? Explain these effects. (p. 686)

36. What is the mechanism of action of the tricyclic antidepressants? (p. 686)

37. What neurochemical hypothesis of depression is suggested by the pharmacological action of the two classes of antidepressant drugs, MAO inhibitors and tricyclic antidepressants? (p. 686)

38. Name an example each of tricyclic antidepressants with more pronounced effect on serotonin and one with greater effect on catecholamines. (p. 687)
    5-HT _____   NE/DA _____

39. What conclusions have been drawn regarding the neurochemical origin of retarded versus agitated depression? (p. 687)

40. Explain why the antidepressant effectiveness of two recently-discovered tricyclic drugs, iprindole and mianserin, casts doubt on the hypothesis that depression results from insufficient activity of monoamine neurons. (p. 687)

41. What experimental evidence suggests that the antidepressant activity of tricyclics is due to their ability to block histamine receptors? (pp. 687-688)

42. What is the mechanism of action of cocaine? Why might we expect it to be an effective antidepressant? (p. 688)

43. What is the effect of intravenous injections of cocaine in depressed versus normal people? (p. 688)

44. Why are these facts about cocaine evidence against the monoaminergic theory of affective disorders? (p. 688)

45. What evidence argues against the histamine hypothesis of affective disorders? (p. 688)

46. Name a drug that can produce depression. _____
What is the mechanism of action of this drug? (p. 688)

47. Why do the emotional effects of reserpine support the monoaminergic insufficiency hypothesis of affective disorders? (pp. 688-689)

<u>Thought</u> <u>Questions</u>

1. Why do you suppose unipolar depression strikes women three times more often then men?

2. Do you think the "normal" emotional ups and downs and the inability to concentrate that we all experience are neurochemically similar to the more extreme cases of schizophrenia and affective psychoses?

The End

Special thanks to Peggy Plant and Jana Standish for their technical help and Wendy Ritger, my editor, for her patience.